LIFE AT THE CAPE

over a hundred years ag

BY A LADY

With contemporary illustrations selected from the work of
THOMAS BOWLER

What this book is about

In August, 1861, a Lady arrived in Cape Town from England. She possessed, apart from a husband and some children, a remarkable talent for observation and a great gift for writing down all she saw and observed. In a controlled style she describes the people she meets and gives her impressions of the country.

She was not much of a stay-at-home; she seems to have been more in the saddle than in a chair, and can therefore say a great deal about the surroundings of the Cape, and her rides to Camps Bay, Kalk Bay, Constantia, Wynberg and Newlands; also about her more ambitious travels to Stellenbosch, Wellington, the Paarl and Worcester.

What she tells is very interesting, especially about social customs. She writes about the 'upper-ten', the old Dutch and the English families, their elegant houses, what they did and did not do, what they ate and drank, their picnic parties and their dance evenings; she also tells about the fishermen, the Malay tailors, and the whole somewhat untidy but colourful scenes of the 'men in the street'.

ACKNOWLEDGEMENTS
We express gratitude to Mr T. Roos and to the Library
of Parliament for permission to reproduce pictures by Thomas
Bowler in the Mendelssohn Collection; also to Miss P. Sellicks,
and to Mr and Mrs F. Bradlow, for all their co-operation and advice.

The text of this book was originally published as a series of letters in the
Cape Monthly Magazine during 1871–1872

Reprints:
1963 (Struik Publishers (Pty) Ltd)
1973 (Struik Publishers (Pty) Ltd)
1983 (Centaur Publishers (Pty) Ltd)

This edition published in 1998 by Struik Publishers (Pty) Ltd
(a member of The Struik New Holland Group of Companies)
Cornelis Struik House
80 McKenzie Street
Cape Town 8001

Reg. No.: 54/00965/07

Copyright © in this edition Struik Publishers (Pty) Ltd 1998

ISBN 1 86872 148 5

Editors: Catherine Mallinick and Joy Clack
Designer: Beverley Dodd

Reproduction by Hirt & Carter Cape (Pty) Ltd
Printed and bound by CTP Book Printers (Pty) Ltd

2 4 6 8 10 9 7 5 3 1

Contents

Illustrations

CHAPTER ONE

First impressions of people and scenery

20th August, 1861

You will be glad to hear of our safe arrival. We landed on a Sunday morning of most dazzling clearness, and were at once struck by the apparent size of the place, the great width of the streets, and the comparatively dwarfed appearance of the double-storied houses and shops – after London and Edinburgh. How we revelled that day in fresh fish for dinner, and unlimited supplies of sparkling water at table! The sky here is intensely blue, and Table Mountain is of marvellous beauty; so, instead of wishing myself back in England, I honestly yearned that day for the society of all old friends, so as to let them share the enjoyment we could not but feel amid scenes and an atmosphere so intensely fresh and exhilirating. The streets were rough and dusty, and the arrangement of 'stoeps' but a poor substitute for good side-pavement on a rainy day. But Cape Town itself is not badly laid out, and it has lovely suburbs, so far as we could make them out from the anchorage. The back of the town is relieved by dark-green forests of pine and bush, and nearly every other house is whitewashed, and with windows shaded by venetian shutters. This gives it quite a continental air.

We have unpacked all our household goods, with but little breakage, and are now beginning to feel the comforts of a settled home. It is surprising what a very 'home' air can be imparted to the barest barrack walls by arranging the treasures and souvenirs collected in one's travels, and you would be delighted with the charming photographs and sketches, which from time to time we have managed to add to our drawing-room screens. *** We found J— entrenched in the Castle (a sort of Tower of London in miniature, much affected by staff-officers and regimental big-wigs) in occupation of a suite of apartments looking on to Table Bay, and commanding a most lovely and extensive sea view.

The hills around us are really Swiss mountains, and we could not have arrived at a better season of the year to revel upon their manifold beauties. Though we are still supposed to be suffering from winter, the trees are everywhere bursting into leaf; and the busy scenes transacting in the waters beneath our quarters (especially when the cormorants are tumbling headlong after the fish, with a great splash) are a never-ending source of amusement. Just now the weather is especially pleasant. We are always out-of-doors; and I sometimes think on a fine sunny day that to my poor weak chest the crisp air is even more joyous and effervescent than laughing gas would be.

As for the scenery about which you inquired, I need scarcely say that Table Bay is *not* so perfect a picture as the Bay of Naples; but it is very well worth seeing, if only for its constant succession of brilliant seascapes, which defy my powers of description, and for the extraordinary wealth of colour in the sunset effects. It would require a Ruskin to attempt to define the brilliant hues pulsating in cloudland here when the sun is about to take his final dip into the sea. It has become quite a favourite drive of ours already, to Sea Point – to view the atmospheric glories raging in tumult over the bed of fiery Phoebus, when the sun has dipped; and instant darkness comes rushing across the land. It is, I assure you, a grand sight to watch the big breakers come tumbling in against the rocks, and contrast their white crests and emerald backs with the deep purple and violet shadows formed in the hollows of miles of charging waves that are roughening the horizon. The children, however, take a more practical interest in the lovely shells encrusting the fine sandy beaches of Green Point, and are mad with delight when they are allowed to pull off their shoes and socks and paddle after the gorgeous sea-flowers blooming in the limpid pools of this rocky coast.

They are already in a fair way of being spoiled by the good-natured bachelors of the regiment, who amuse themselves by teaching Charles and Freddie how to catch 'harders' and 'klipfish', *et hoc genus omne*, off the wharves and jetties running into Table Bay. The fish seem quite fearless and play about in shoals under the keels of the cargo-boats; as the water is very clear you can follow all their movements with the greatest ease. The soldiers are great fellows for angling, and at any hour of the day you may see them dashing the 'grains' into the dazzling masses of 'harders', and landing three or four of these silvery mackerel at every cast. It is a very pretty sight, too, to go down to the Central Causeway any afternoon about three o'clock and watch the fleet of fishing-boats coming to the anchorage after a hard day's toil at hooking 'snoek', 'silverfish', 'hottentot', 'stumpnose', and 'geelbeck'. There they come in a long double file, rounding the end of the North Jetty, their white sails glittering in the sun, their crews toiling at their oars in measured sweep; while boat after boat, as it reaches the smooth water of the haven, folds its white wings, lowers its mast, and is rushed up the beach by the stalwart arms of the half-naked coolies, who dash into the surf to steady the gunwales, and promote an early delivery of their varied hauls.

It would also do your heart good to see the crowds of healthy children swarming in the Fish-market when these boats have been hastily emptied! Such lively, jovial imps in bronze, tugging away at huge, yard-long monsters of fish, and wrangling with true Southern vivacity over the proprietorship of each capacious two-pennyworth of scaly matter as it is bundled into baskets, only require a painter of a humorous turn, to fill you with admiration of the quaint grace and beauty of form to be met with among the '*polloi*' and street Arabs of our colonial population. There is nothing funnier to be seen than the peculiar method of dispatching 'snoek' as soon as caught. As these monstrous pikes, sometimes four feet long, are armed with terrible sharp teeth, the fishermen are provided with a small club with which to stun them by a blow on the nose the moment they are drawn out of the sea. They therefore have a large number of lines hanging over the gunwales of the boats, and it is diverting to watch them from the Castle ramparts, pulling up the fish as fast as they can, tucking them up like helpless babies under their left arms with one jerk of the wrist, and followed by an immediate tap on the head or nose with the club. The boatmen thus seem to be always performing the antics of Punch and Judy for our especial entertainment; and nay breezy day you may see dozens of these boats fishing among the shipping in Table Bay, and all of them doing a capital business, I am sure.

26th August.— Like many better-known places, Cape Town has its share of privileged simpletons, and is unusually rich in sable specimens of harmless lunacy. The natives here, like their brethren in the East, regard a madman as something sacred, and you cannot pass a week in Cape Town without stumbling across dwarfs as deformed as the cripple in Raphael's cartoon, or without being spoken to by the funny old creature who rejoices in the *sobriquet* of 'Queen Rebecca'. Poor wretch! she may be harmless enough, but she can make herself horribly offensive by her gibberings and grimaces. Fail to give her fair words or a bit of silver, and her hideous majesty will pour out a flood of incoherent jargon, wherein she descants upon the peculiar peccadilloes of every local worthy in a manner and with a fluency that is positively electrifying. Poor old Queen! you ought long ago to have been sent to the Robben Island Institute! You are the embodiment of Monsieur Du Chaillu's dream of the civilized gorilla, and would be a great addition to the Regent's Park menagerie! She and I frequently meet when I am out shopping or lunching at Cairncross's, and we have quite struck up a platonic friendship, and I hope in my next to amuse you with some of her wonderful confessions.

The streets, indeed, are full of picturesque 'bits', and every idle corner attracts me strangely by its superfluity of dramatic incident. To see the boys chaffering with the fruit hawkers is as good as a play; and the solemn air with which the long-robed Mohammedan priest paces his way through the crowds of Malay lazzaroni, graciously receiving their salutes and salaams, speaks volumes for his self-respect. Here the British soldier and the blue-coated policeman change positions entirely, as the knights of the truncheon seem less popular with the cookmaids, are very stiff and unbending, and are sharply looked after by their inspectors and sergeants, who are generally well mounted, and not unlike staff officers in appearance. The soldiers, on the contrary, are very lightly attired in canvas 'jumpers' or linen tunics, and seem to be hand-in-glove with innumerable acquaintances. As for the officers, they are always in mufti. *** Everybody dresses in the fashion he likes best; and you seldom meet people with black or tawby faces who are not admirably in keeping with the bright colours and pictorial arrangements of their fluttering rags.

This country, indeed, should be the paradise of painters, for nowhere could you witness more delicate aerial effects, or find more exquisite gradations of colour in rock and bush, sky and scenery, than in South Africa. To you who have been always accustomed to see sunshine veiled in mist, it would be a new sensation to gaze with the unaided eye upon the granite buttresses of Table Mountain, or the sharply-defined peaks of such serrated ranges as the blue mountains of Hottentots' Holland, many miles distant, and mark the tender blending of greys and greens, of purples and pinks, that in infinite variety of tint bloom from every crevice and scaur, every crag and ravine, upon those inhospitable Southern Alps.

There is, for instance, the Devil's Peak – a perfect poem in itself, as it rises grandly over the military lines, and hems in the south-eastern arm of the great semicircle within which Cape Town is compressed. This wing of Table Mountain is a perfect art study. It is beautifully shaped. It stands out boldly against the sky-line. It is a perfect battle-ground for the winds; but no photograph that I can send you can give any idea of the shifting lights and shadows, which the course of the sun develops out of its rocky masses and well-clothed spurs, as the dawn and the day, the noon and the night successively melt into each other. Its sides and gullies are full of proteas, heaths, and silver trees. Here cascades leap and bushes shiver as the fierce north-westers crash down upon those heights and make the foliage change from emerald to opal at every successive blast. At one moment its jagged crests are swallowed up in vapour, then a whirl of wind, and the fleecy masses are torn into shreds and sent howling over the precipices in tortuous eddies. Anon the whole mountain becomes deep purple as the sun is obscured, only to break out again into wealth of colour as the passing cloud has melted into thin air. Thus the mixture of clay, granite, and lichened stones, cropping out everywhere in those

wind-tormented heights, is beautifully toned down and brought into harmony with surrounding objects, by the fusion and contrast of every tint of green and purple which bush, rock, or flower individually furnish.

If England, or even Scotland, contained such lovely mountains as these, who would care to follow a marching regiment abroad? But life in our colonies is indeed far from being very miserable, if we only agree to forget the heartburnings and strivings after effect which are entailed upon the higher, if not better, classes of the mother country, by reason of their exceeding wealth and worldly or social advantages. Any family with a moderate fixed income cannot fail, I feel convinced, to secure an immense deal of healthy entertainment by arranging to spend some years at the Cape. It is not alone that the climate is so pleasant, and the necessaries, and even the luxuries, of life are so cheap; but the people themselves are so exceedingly kind-hearted and well-bred that one is only sorry that they are, as a body, so poor, and not very likely to grow rich in a hurry.

The coloured people, especially, are surprisingly polite. Insolence and surliness seem banished from their homes; and in their intercourse with strangers Cape Malays would set a bright example to many English provincials. In the so-called society of the place there is no sharply-defined line between class and class; and, as a rule, you will meet with quieter, well-bred manners among the necessarily mixed lot who attend the subscription balls than you would expect to find among people who are engaged in trade, and have but few opportunities of studying the habits of really first-class circles. I presume this is due to the republican and Huguenot sentiments imported here from Holland and France by the early settlers and political refugees, and by the long existence of the domestic institution in a modified form. At all events, I have been charmed by the glimpses which I have been permitted to catch of Cape ladies in their own homes. *** Though their leaning is not towards intellectual exertion, they are extremely courteous, and thoroughly disinterested in their hospitalities, and when we leave this station, we shall leave many very pleasant native-born acquaintances behind us.

The ladies here have a very excellent plan of calling upon all desirable strangers within a week after new arrivals have been seen in church. This enables the ladies of the garrison especially to make a rapid acquaintance, if they are so minded, with the proverbial hospitality of Cape residents; and I assure you it is surprising how very well-ordered are the appointments of many of these houses. They are generally situated in the suburbs – called the 'Gardens', – and besides being provided with stables and coach-houses, have flower-plots and verandahs loaded with bloom. Most of the drawing-rooms are very prettily furnished, with profusion of vases, easy chairs and walnut and rosewood articles 'de luxe'; and nearly all the people who have called upon me are to be envied the fresh-smelling bouquets of wild or English hothouse flowers that so becomingly deck their tables and windows. They always laugh at my enthusiastic love of flowers, and especially smile at my passion for the 'arum', which grows in all the ditches under the title of 'pig-lily', and reaches an enormous size. But you have only to hint that flowers or fruit cannot be purchased to have as many nosegays sent to you as your heart can desire. In this particular, I must say, they are exceedingly liberal.

Of course, it is just possible that in your mind's eye you picture me as panting with heat, choked with dust, and utterly *ennuyed* by the conversation of the garrison hacks who crowd around the whitewashed walls of some wretched barrack hovel allowed us by a liberal War Office. And there is no doubt, from what Lady S— tells me, that the Commandant's quarters can very easily in summer be made too hot to hold anybody, so small and so close are the two yards or quadrangles upon which all the rooms of the Castle officials open; but then the sea breeze makes amends for many *desagremens* common to all barrack accommodation; and we can always go and live up in the Gardens, under the cool shadow of old Table Mountain, or nestle in winter in one of the many snug cottages fringing the southern suburbs. Besides, we have received so many invitations to spend a week at Wynberg, Rondebosch, Stellenbosch, &c., all within easy distance of Cape Town, that we are not going to make ourselves miserable, if we can help it, before our time. As yet croquet has not taken deep root among the Cape ladies. The want of lawns is probably the cause of it; but picnics, with music and dancing, are no unpleasant substitute, and the sands of Camp's Bay and the woods of Mr. Breda are never long deserted by the mirthful throng.

Any fresh arrival with a little singing talent is soon regarded as a great acquisition; for although the colonial-born ladies are capital horsewomen, and espeically strong in the dancing line, they are not given to the drudgery which good music demands. For one who can sing with judgement, science, and expression, you will find dozens who can dance uninterruptedly from the opening of a ball to its close, viz., from nine to four, and this even without disarranging their 'coiffure'. Musical parties are thus an especial treat, and generally furnish the quidnuncs with gossip for a week. All simple ballad music is deservedly honoured, and the clever natives soon pick up the most complicated operatic overtures, and after one hearing at a concert, will whistle the score, in capital time, of nearly every piece that has taken their fancy. They are admirable mimics, and especially clever with the violin and the accordion, playing entirely by the ear. It is quite a treat to hear them whistling in roving quartette bands on fine moonlight evenings, each man in subjection to his mates. Their accuracy is surprising!

1st September.— It is time I told you about my pets! Although we have been scarcely settled here a month, J— has succeeded in buying me a beautiful little bay, and is himself the owner of a handsome chestnut charger, which latter, when not otherwise engaged on parade, is frequently put into the Cape pleasure cart, which he has purchased for forty guineas, and made to convey us all over the country. Although I can't say much for the state of the roads, the children enjoy immensely these pleasure trips to the Flats, Cape Downs, and Green Point, and I think the jolting improves all our digestions. A Cape cart is quite a colonial institution. It is a highly-decorated dog-cart, with seats capable of being reversed, as in a mail phaeton, and covered with a painted canvas hood, sunblinds in front and rear, and supplied with side curtains like a Hampton Court van. These carts are very light and very strong. They resist the rain, the sun, and dust, and are just the thing for a country where everyone passes three fourths of his day and time in the open air. Many of J—'s brother officers sport their wagonettes, or let their wives dash about in basket phaetons; but I prefer the Cape cart, as being in every way more convenient and more suited to the climate. They are frequently driven curricle fashion with two horses; but one horse is quite enough to satisfy our moderate tastes. The ladies here ride very fairly. In fact, although our English habits are much better cut and fit more exquisitely as a rule than any that I have yet seen proceed from any Cape Town tailors, yet the lithe slender forms of the young girls lend themselves gracefully to the bounding action of their well-bred hacks; and they appear as fearless of their spirited pets as if they were schoolboys home for the holidays. All the gentlemen appear to ride well. They look better on horseback than a-foot, and are, I fancy, very fond of 'chopping and changing', which taste implies some knowledge of horseflesh.

My own dear little 'Sunbeam' is a perfect little fellow, about 14 hands high, with legs of iron and a pair of bold, saucy, black eyes, that stand about an inch out of his head. Never was there seen so perfectly well-trained a creature! He is the cleverest and the handsomest of his kind, and would be worth 150 guineas in England. He cost us £35! Though anything but nervous, he is such a funny, impulsive little man, that it always makes me laugh to watch the lively twitching, backwards and forwards, of his pointed little Arab ears, whenever, in a riding party, any of my accompanying cavaliers' horses are imprudent enough to press beyond us, ever so slightly, in the canter. In a moment, poor 'Sunbeam' arches his neck, snorts defiance, glances fiercely at his neighbours, and strains against the bit, till every vein in his body seems to tingle and swell with suppressed fury. His action, always high, becomes more and more *prononcé*. His hoofs seem to spurn the very ground, as *ventre à terre* he bounds up the hill, his tail standing stiffly out, a foe to all compromise! Of course, his neighbours increase the pace as 'Sunbeam' increases his own; and before we know where we are, we are racing away for dear life; and my sides ache from laughter at 'Sunbeam's' impatient, jealous snaps of the teeth, to prevent being passed by his fleeter companions.

Our favourite ride is round the Kloof. This roadway has been constructed by the military by the orders of old Sir Harry Smith, and is cut out of the base of the Lion's Head and Hill – which form the north-western boundary of Cape Town. It is about nine miles long, and is, to my mind, a more beautiful road than the far-famed 'Queen's Drive', round the base of Arthur's Seat at Edinburgh. The road gradually ascends for three miles, and is carried by numerous curves and windings over a kloof, which separates the Lion's Head from Table Mountain, until you reach a tableland, when you get magnificent and extensive views of the town and bay, and also of the broad Atlantic, stretching away into infinitude of space. You have thus within a few yards of plateau no less than four extensive prospects, as you glance at the four points of the compass; and I am not yet decided which view is really the most picturesque. The road then gradually descends for three miles more, skirting at a considerable height the rocky shores of Camp's Bay, until you finally reach the villa-crowned heights of Sea Point and Green Point, whence a sharp canter of twenty minutes will bring you back to the town again. Throughout the whole of this lovely drive the scenery is of the most diversified character, alike reminding you of the Glencoe Hills, the Via Mala, and the least rugged parts of the Simplon; and I am never tired of scampering up the Kloof to see the sun set, and admire the powerful contrast between the rugged features of the Lion's Head and the western triangular side of Table Mountain.

Should a sharp south-easter be blowing heavily in the town, not a breath of wind will reach you on the solemn braes of the Kloof, though the clouds in heavy, fleecy masses will be pouring over the hills, and ruffling in stormy gusts the squadrons of marine cavalry, as they hoarsely come charging on to the beach of Camp's Bay, with trumpets braying, pennons waving, and their plumy crests foaming in the breeze. Ah! what delicious moments of satisfaction are those, when we view the whole horizon rendering homage to the sinking sun, and the glowing clouds seem symbolical of the perfect happiness reigning in the regions of the blest! Then comes a short, delightful, poetic after-glow. Darkness wells up from the sea like a rising river, and embraces us in its folds. As we pause upon these heights, the hum of insects and the chirping of crickets are rendered shriller and keener by the mournful silence of the solemn solitude; the scent of the 'avond bloemetjies' is fragrant in the air and with careful rein and hushed remarks, we gradually pick our way back again to our quarters in the Castle.

It is curious how few people we meet on these charming heights. Beyond a few Malays returning from a fishing excursion to the rocks in Camp's Bay, armed with rods and lines of a portentous length, you seldom pass a soul. Of course there is no traffic, – it would be desecration: but still one would expect that this drive would have been the haunt of all the ball-room fairies, whom we meet with, however, in the more congenial grounds of the Botanical Gardens, decked in muslins and ravishing bonnets. These

Gardens, I must tell you, are quite a feature in Cape Town life. They are not unlike Kew and Kensington, and generally are crowded with well-dressed people, to listen to the regimental band on fine days. They are placed on the right-hand side of the long avenue of massive oak trees which leads up to the private grounds of Government-house, and are kept in most admirable order by a thorough brither Scot, who is kindness itself to inquisitive strangers. There must be something peculiar in the air of the Cape, to make people so kind and disinterested, or else we are considered unusual specimens of humanity. When a party of officers got up a ball, not very many nights ago, all the rare exotics and hot-house plants, freshening the supper table, were gratuitously supplied by the superintendent of these Gardens: and you have only to express a love for scenery, and half of your acquaintance are ready to show you over the country, that you may see and admire.

Apropos of this, there are many fine trees growing here, derived from Australia, which I should think would suit your garden and lawn. For instance, the blackwood is a tall, pyramidical tree, not unlike a beech in its compact foliage, but infinitely more graceful and feathery in its branchings. It spreads out like a yew tree, and grows to a great size in twelve years. Many gentlemen plant a couple in front of their stoeps, as it always is in leaf, and a great deal handsomer than the poplars, which the Dutch residents brought with them from Holland, and still stick to conservatively. The blue-gums also seem thorougly acclimatized to the Cape, and on the road to Rondebosch they rear their lofty heads in nearly every hedge and garden. You would be greatly charmed with the silver tree, of whose leaves I will send you a whole hatful next mail, that you may exercise your ingenuity in working up their silky, velvety, leathery tongues of silver into Christmas ornaments, wreaths, and book-markers. I wish you could see the variety of wild flowers, and the excessive size and beauty of the waxy-leaved camellias growing in the open air. Fuchsias, geraniums, and verbenas are as common as weeds; and the number and exquisite delicacy of the lilies and bulbs are only to be equalled by the fantastic modelling and colouring of the native heaths. Even the very commons are gay with the oxalis tribe. But a truce to these rambling sentiments, ere I drive you into the desperation born of hopeless envy.

8th September.— Our shopping, you will be pleased to hear, is very complete. 'Fletcher's' is our Cape 'Marshall & Snelgrove', and they will supply you at their mammoth establishment in Keizersgracht with anything in haberdashery, from a button to brussels lace. Their shop, or series of shops, comprises the sale of everything essential to household expenditure, except bread, meat, and drink; and the mixture of articles is very 'bizarre'. Then there are cheap Jacks, who almost take your breath away by the astounding manner in which they advertise their wares, previously purchased for a mere bagatelle at the public auctions, which are held every Saturday on the Parade grounds: and what is very curious, many of these articles are really very good of their kind. We see the effect in the wonderful variety of hue and material in which the native women array themselves. Shawls and prints gay enough to startle the primitive colours out of the field, give an animation and sparkle to the streets of Cape Town, that might be otherwise wanting in our so-called 'snuff-and-butter' brethren of the south.

The Malays, especially, are very fond of rich personal adornment, and affect a peculiar mode of dress, somewhat in the style of the mezzotinto engravings of our grandmothers, where the waist was placed under the arm-pits, and the roundness of the barrel-like figure was created out of innumerable highly-starched petticoats, or series of gowns. A Malay beauty trusts largely to the smoothness and glossy sheen of her well-greased hair. She smears it well with cocoanut butter, brushes it tightly from her forehead, *a la imperatrice*, and twists the back hair into coils so tight, that she looks as if she could never shut her eyes again. She either minces upon neat satin 'bottes', or clatters upon '*caparrans*' (a species of wooden buskin), and it is marvellous how firmly they can keep their footing upon these comical pattens: her shoulders are draped a la Marie Antoinette by a very vivid-patterned kerchief; and a big gold skewer through her ebony chignon completes her holiday bravery. The *tout ensemble* is very picturesque and highly odorous!

On the other hand, the Malay swells, especially on Fridays, which is their Sabbath, shave their heads scrupulously, and never go uncovered. They always keep their scalps warm with bright cotton kerchiefs, and wear over them a triangular pagoda style of hat, manufactured out of straw in the Colony. Vest, coat, and trowsers are of cloth or merino, and seldom of the same tint. I have seen them in green, blue, yellow, brown, and olum colours, and such little linen as they use is unexceptionably white and clean. The impression they make at first sight is very agreeable; their manners are quiet and gentlemanly, their voices soft and musical, and they are remarkably sober and industrious, with serious, sedate countenances. Our groom, Achmat, gets £3 a month and finds himself, and he manages, too, on that to support a wife and two little miniatures of himself; so that it is quite clear he must be thrifty in his housekeeping.

I hear a good many ladies rail against their servants, and here, as in England, mistresses get much trouble out of their 'followers'; but, after all, they are a great deal better suited than they will admit. The native servants, at all events, don't drink; they are extremely civil, and are very much attached to their young charges; and if you don't object to their colonial dishes, I consider the cooking to be a great deal better than plain roast and boiled, of which I am heartily tired. Their chief fault seems to be forgetfulness of orders; and they are very fond of holidays. Scarcely a month have we had Achmat with us, and he has already asked permission to attend three funerals of relatives and a couple of weddings; and if we were to refuse, he would simply take French leave, and his successor would follow in his footsteps. Considering the fact that these Malays were once all slaves, it is not to be wondered at that they now enjoy their freedom, and have resolved to banish from their faces and thoughts all trace of anxious servility. You never see them weep. They are forbidden by the Koran to mourn their dead; and like the Epicureans of old, they esteem that man happiest who bothers himself least with his own concerns or those of his neighbours.

We have only been to two balls as yet, one given by the Artillery and one at Government-house. The latter was very crowded; and although the rooms are large and the Governor's aides-de-camp most attentive to strangers, still to find partners for 300 people, all wanting to dance at the same time, must have severely tried their courtesy, and made it very difficult for us to see much of the dresses or criticize the company fairly. One thing struck me at once, and that was, the absence of giggle and *gaucherie* amongst the daughters of the middle-class gentry there assembled. The naval 'bucks', as usual, were here, there, and everywhere, and slightly boisterous in their hearty appreciation of fun and supper; but otherwise the behaviour of everyone was everything to be desired. Certainly, the Cape girls are indefatigable waltzers; and they had the good sense to dress in nice, becoming, fresh tarlatans and gauzy gowns, instead of vieing with each other in expensive silks and satins. Many of the chaperons and married women were, of course, disposed on the benches running round the ball-room, but except in the fact of being more richly and carefully dressed, they seemed to me to be not a whit less fresh and lively than the frisky youngsters in the lancers or galop. The climate is so dry that ladies soon lose that peachiness and bloom of skin peculiar to colder countries, but they do not age so rapidly, and I think, on the whole, they have a very good time of it. The music was alternately played by a military brass and by a native string band, and I greatly preferred the latter.

The Governor, Sir G—, is very fond of seeing young people enjoy themselves, and appears to thoroughly appreciate his popularity with the fair sex. He mixes freely in the crowd, and has a kind word for everyone; and it is easy to see how completely he identifies himself with the mixed races over whom he has been called to rule. Everybody speaks well of him, and you never hear an ill-natured remark levelled against the Viceroy's Court and its doings.

I must now break off, and trust by next mail that I will have a long budget of home news from you, upon which to comment and grow sentimental.

CHAPTER TWO

Lovely and sequestered Camps Bay

21st September, 1861

It is too bad! Here has the mail come in, and not a line from you to tell how all the old folk at home are getting on in our absence! Considering that we are only a month's voyage apart, I think you might have been a little more considerate to the poor exile, and done your utmost to cheer her melancholy star. *** And yet, after all, I dare say, I am a great deal better off and happier at this present moment than you probably imagine. I am staying here for a week with a most delightful family, to whom our friends in Yorkshire were good enough to give us letters of introduction, and from whom we have received such unaffected acts of spontaneous kindness as we never can repay.

Naturally, you will ask: Where is Camp's Bay? and what are you doing there? and what on earth can make the — family take such an interest in your amusement? To all of which I reply: 'Wait a bit *mon ami*, and you will hear in good time!'

Camp's Bay, then, is a most lovely and sequestered little bay, within six miles' ride from Cape Town, and ought to be the future Brighton of the Cape. It lies at the back of Table Mountain, is almost deserted, and beyond the smoke ascending from a couple of farm-houses and the patches of corn near some shepherds' huts, bears scarcely any trace of man's presence. It was, nevertheless, once the favourite sea-side residence of Lord Charles Somerset, from whose admitted good taste and judgment, in planting trees and breeding horses, the Cape has derived incalculable benefit. Here the queer old Viceroy was wont to recruit his wasted energies, and obtain some freedom from that care and worry which are always incident to a public man's life; and here, too, he laid the foundation, it is said, of much of the ill-fame that is never altogether absent from the *roue* and the despot. Be this as it may, Camp's Bay House is now shorn of its former glories, and is almost hidden from riders on the Kloof Road by the thick plantation of stone-pines which shelters it from the rude blasts of the south-east winds. The —'s still say that in November month the wind blows with such violence as to pluck their cabbages out of the ground, and toss their garden soil into clouds of fine dust; but though all stories of this kind should be taken *cum grano salis*, I am afraid the bay is very open indeed to the assaults of hurricane gusts, and to fierce tornados from the overhanging cliffs.

What brought us here was simply this; — Rosalie contracted an obstinate cold, and Dr. B. (a very kind, pleasant little man, as all good doctors ought to be) strongly advised us to get away from the Castle ditch, avoid medicine, and get her change, either to Camp's Bay or to the Somerset Strand, with plenty of sea-bathing and fresh milk, &c., &c. When we mentioned our letters to the —'s, he kindly offered to see them upon the subject, and next day we got a hearty invitation to bring the little maid with us, as soon as we liked, if we were not afraid of roughing it. As Dr. B. would hear of no denial, James rode over, and was so charmed with the hearty manner of his reception, that we did not hesitate in forty-eight hours to plant ourselves on the hospitality of people, who only knew us by the good officers of others in no way related to them, and I have never once regretted the tremendous boldness of that step, so very significant of colonial ways and means. Behold us, then, fairly settled in our impromptu home, surrounded by good books, pictures, and abundance of music to add zest to the secluded life and charming solitude of this delightfully healthy spot! The house itself is a long range of barrack-like rooms, opening by French windows to the ground, and capable of accommodating with ease three or four families. The court is gay with flowers, and the verandahs are fragrant with honeysuckle and monthly roses, but the wind sadly deranges any attempt to get up a conservatory, the cherished ambition of our accomplished and amiable hostess.

Every morning, since I got here, I have been up by five o'clock to see the weird-like effects of dawn breaking on the hills, and after the refreshment of a delicious cup of strong coffee, to take the youngsters down to bathe. How you would enjoy the long stretch of hard, smooth, white beach, where the waves come gently peeping over the edge, and then hoarsely retiring again among the rocks! Here the children join hands in the tiny, clear waves, and dance about most joyously, but I don't allow them to stay too long in the water, as it is intensely cold and *stinging with brine*, and they are all the colours of the rainbow when they emerge. But after five minutes' scampering on the beach, and half an hour spent in hunting for shells, crabs, and sea-weed, or any of the hundred-and-one delights that abound here, as they do at Bournemouth or at Ilfracombe, the big bell summons us to breakfast, and we hurry up with *such* appetites, that I am sure we must be trenching sadly on the hospitality of our kind hosts, but they never seem to think we can take *half* enough to please them. Old Mr.— has been a great traveller in his day, and tells us wonderful stories of his experiences on the frontier and in the Free State, in days when life in the Colony was much less settled than it is now, and it is a great pity his family cannot induce him to put on paper some of the more exciting memoirs of his own youth. He is a fair specimen of what a good colonist should be – wiry, persevering, full of pluck, not daunted by trouble, and yet with a sly leaning to the resources of literature, where least you would expect it. As for his wife – fancy Aunt M— with a dash of E—s' bashfulness, and you can easily imagine how well we get on together.

There is a fine fir wood behind the house, which ought to be a great blessing during the approaching hot months, and where we retire every morning after the gentlemen of the family have driven over to Cape Town on business – or else bask and simmer in the pleasant sunshine under the verandah; alternatively working, reading, or chatting, but wasting most of my time, lying idly back in my chair, – *blinking at the flies*, and drinking in the quiet beauty of the scene. Such colouring! – such shifting shades of green and purple, – such very green waves and such very white sands; such very bold, big black rocks and boulders – breaking the skyline, and causing the spray to be dashed over them in lofty sheets of vapour, – that one's eyes become fairly dazzled with the excessive purity of the fresh air and sunshine! No need for careful toilet, no unnecessary anxiety as to boots or gloves! We have no neighbours within a mile of us, and if we had, they would not care a bit! This is a free country, and we can do what we like – so we *just please ourselves*, and enjoy the *dolce far niente*, reckless of Fashion, and only waiting on Health. Whenever a tiny wreath of smoke blots the blue horizon, we all run for telescopes; and for another hour watch its gradual growth and progress, as if our lives depended on it – till at last some long-looked-for steamer heaves into sight, and passes so close that we can distinctly make out people on the deck. We hoist a red flag – dip it, and hoist it up again, and of course our salute is courteously acknowledged in the same fashion. Small coasting vessels are frequently sighted by us, and a regular fleet of fishing boats are ever on the move in the offing. We hear, too, of porpoises and whales, but have seen none as yet.

23rd September.— Yesterday afternoon, being Sunday, we took a glorious stroll up the hills behind us, and so over to the 'Round-House' Gardens – (which are famous for their almonds and fruit trees, and a great resort for Cape cockneys on high days and holidays). In the course of our walk we gathered heaps of wild flowers, as their numbers and luxuriance are simply irresistible. Out of great bunches of a heathery shrub, (which I am told is rather uncommon elsewhere, but which here abounds with its white and fragrant little stars), aided by *waxy* evergreens, the bright blue wild lobelias, a lovely *mauve* flower that grows in masses, pipettes of *woolly scarlet* heath, a frond or two of scented geranium, and a handful of the long trailing sprays of a creeper called *'Love lies bleeding'* – in a few minutes, we soon made up bouquets enough to brighten every room in the Castle! Don't you envy us our belongings? *** Then, just as the sun was about to dip, we sat us down to rest on the margin of the Upper Kloof Road, and then witnessed such a glorious sunset as I never shall forget. Barred with ragged streaks of cloud, the glowing sun kept revolving through them like a fiery globe at white heat, scorching them into flame, and leaving smirches of blood in the sky as it rolled on its downward path, dyeing the rosy heavens with the reflection from a sea of glory. Soon piles of little clouds flushed into gold, crimson, pale olive, and bronze, rapidly changing and fusing into purple and pink, and a most wonderful, delicate greenish hue, which I had always believed to be an impossible tint in cloudland, and only to be seen in dreams of heavenly bliss. Half fascinated with the scene, I was fairly astonished at the singular effect of such a sunset upon the surrounding mountains. They appeared to be *red hot and almost transparent*, – so thoroughly were the rocks and buttresses fused in the haze and sunny dust of reflected light. However, night came rushing upon as at such a tremendous pace, that we soon had to leave so much beauty, for fear we might lose both our supper and the path, if we did not hurry quickly home. These effects only last a few minutes; but then what enjoyment is there not crowded into these exquisite moments! The flashing and flushing of warm colour in the sky produce an extraordinary impression, and are quite as lovely in their way as the Aurora Borealis in your colder North.

25th September.— To give you an idea of the open-air life we are just now leading, I don't suppose any one in the house is ever without his or her hat on, except at bed-time and at meals. The children are up to their eyes in seaweed and shells, and getting burned as brown as berries. As for myself, I could not really work, if I were flogged for my laziness; and it is much better fun making friends with the four-footed pets of the house than cultivating the mysteries of crochet. These dogs are respectively called 'X', 'Y', and 'Z', from some strange freak of fancy as to the shape of their legs, and are clever enough to use up the whole alphabet in tricks. 'Y' is especially 'spry' at getting into mischief, and made us laugh immensely today by coolly capsizing his young mistress when starting for a ride. Just as she was hustling the steady old cart-horse across the sands, with the whole posse of dogs running ahead to chase up the *'sand-hoppers'*, poor 'Y' suddenly squatted down in her path, to think, and scratch his ears for refreshment – reckless of consequences. Of course, the old horse went head and heels over him, and set his fair rider sprawling; and it was comical to see the old rogue come trotting home sulkily, his thick lips hanging, and every bit of curl frightened out of his tail. Equally as a matter of course, little Miss— picked herself up, backed her steed against a rock, and scrambled into her saddle again, as if nothing unusual had happened. And it is in this way, I presume, Cape girls acquire their confident seat on horseback, alternately falling and picking themselves up. Nothing can be more primitive, and it must be capital exercise. In fact, no better plan could be devised than putting a young girl on to a rough but quiet old screw, picked up for a few pounds at last Saturday's sale, and taking it for granted that the two will jolt themselves into harmony with each other.

Mr.—'s Scotch groom was even more primitive in his stable management than the average English emigrant. On the previous Monday he applied for the place, vacant by his predecessor having taken it into his head that Camp's Bay was too retired; and in answer to all inquiries as to his special fitness for the post, Sandy could only give one answer: '*He could na just say he could do this or that, but he was willing; and he was a "hondy mon"*!' So he engaged on a month's trial, and told to go and saddle up the pony for Miss— at once. In about ten minutes he led the creature forth, with the pommel of the saddle *facing the tail*, and the clumsy watering bridle doing duty for curb and snaffle. The poor fellow looked much discomfited at the peals of laughter that greeted him from all sides; and scratching his head in a very contemplative manner, while the error was being rectified, sagely observed, 'Well, he *had* thought there was summut queer, but he could not be expected to know *everything*'. However, I have no doubt Sandy will soon be clever enough, if he will only take his correction in good part, and abstain from being argumentative.

We had a further specimen of his knowledge of horses yesterday, when it was arranged that we should take the dog-cart and drive in to town, to see the Horticultural Exhibition. After breakfast, we had the horses brought to the door, but nothing could induce one of them (a stumpy grey cob) to budge an inch from it. There we sat like a couple of sacks, while everything suggested was being tried by turns. Sandy's bright idea it was to 'span in' the old riding pony in front of the jibber, and haul him off his legs; but as it would have been easier to harness him in his place altogether, that idea was abandoned. He then proposed to take off the brute's bridle, and *let him fancy* he was at liberty to run away up the hill, the steepness of the road being quite sufficient to stop him when out of breath; but as this would have involved an unnecessary dash of danger, that also was put aside. Eventually, the 'hondy mon' tied a riem round the right fetlock, got a purchase round a fir tree, and aided by shouts, whipping, and Highland anathemas, succeeded in getting up the steam! How we did rock and roll about, to be sure! – the road being very narrow, the sides very steep, and no rails or wall to prevent one being toppled over by a sudden swerve! Fortunately, Mr.— was a good whip, and brought us back again all safe; but I think you would have laughed had you met us careering along on that lonely spot – the Kloof Road.

The flowers exhibited were very good of their kind, but I missed the roses we are elsewhere accustomed to. Azaleas, and camellias, and calceolarias attracted the most attention; and there were some beautiful stands of cut flowers – both hot-house and wild. The exhibition yard was thronged with well-dressed people, and altogether we spent a very pleasant day, criticizing the horses, the sheep, and the vegetables. Later in the year, I am told, there will be a capital show of fruit.

26th September.— We were roused up earlier than usual this morning by the merry sounds of music and loud voices before our bed-room windows.

While we were sleeping early bands of Malays had arrived to spend the day in our neighbourhood and enjoy themselves in their own simple *al fresco* fashion under our very walls. There were at least fifty of them gathered together on the beach, hunting up dry bushes, collecting driftwood, and starting fires for coffee-making. The older men dispersed themselves about the rocks to catch soles and 'klipfish', while the younger and more enthusiastic fry incontinently laid themselves out for dancing and a thorough day's enjoyment. How the fiddles did squeak, and the drums and big violoncellos keep thumping away and droning out the most inspiriting strains! In and out, round and round, backward and forward, surged the crowd; footing it and capering, backing and filling,

stamping time, and slapping hands and thighs as the music and the measure kept steadily increasing in pace and fury! Never were there seen more indefatigable dancers! The American Nigger 'breakdowns' were fools to them; and I am sure they richly deserved the appetite and meals which the sea-breeze and the bay were likely to procure them. Through the whole livelong day these people were dancing on the sands, and if ever musicians deserved their beer, these native fiddlers did! Mrs.— sent to ask whether they wanted anything; but beyond a little salt, and a few onions and a bucket or two of fresh clear water from the well, they were absolutely independent of us. In fact, we profited by their presence, as they sent us some excellent 'soles' in exchange; and these 'soles', let me tell you, are most delicious eating. After luncheon, yielding to the invitation of the boys of the house, and hoping to escape the noise and romping of our vivacious visitors, I accompanied them in the boat to an inlet of the sea a little further on. We took a big net with us, and when we arrived at the fishing grounds it was startling to look over the boat's side and gaze through the clear water upon the abundant animal and vegetable life surging and teeming in the sands and over the pebbles beneath us.

The water was as smooth and as translucent as a looking-glass, and it was highly diverting to watch the net sink slowly and steadily down some twenty feet or so till it rested upon bright shells and gleaming sand, and to note the curious way in which the fish swarmed over and around it, evidently lost in astonishment at the strange black thing suddenly arrived in their domain; but presently one little bold 'klipfish', gleaming in bronze armour, came nibbling at the bait, and soon communicated its pleasant flavour to his anxious friends, for in less than five minutes hundreds of these colonial 'whitebait' (who would be delicious but for their numerous spines) swarmed into the toils, and richly rewarded us for our trouble in bringing them to grief. Our landing was not quite so easily effected as our embarkation. By the time we returned the rising tide had submerged the greater part of the rock from which we had started, and the freshening breeze took a mean advantage of us, and caused two innocent-looking waves to break completely over us and our boat, and drench us most ignominiously. However, all is well that ends well; and the Malays came readily to our assistance, and speedily got the seine and its contents to shore.

And now our visit is drawing to a close. I cannot tell you how sorry I shall be at having to say good-bye tomorrow. Rosalie is looking ever so much better, and I am sure I can never repay the — family the deep debt of obligation under which they have placed us during our stay. Money can never measure the delight of receiving disinterested services from thoroughly good people; and it is a delight to me that by singing and sketching I have been enabled to impart some slight degree of pleasure entertainment to friends who are so charming in their manners and gifted with such great natural refinement.

CHAPTER THREE

An old-fashioned house in the Gardens

5th October, 1861

S ince the date of my last, we have had an addition to the garrison, and have been obliged to turn out of our free quarters to make way for greater swells than ourselves; so, upon the principle of 'Excelsior', we have gone up in the social scale by ascending to the delectable regions of the 'Gardens', and consider ourselves extremely fortunate in securing a ready-furnished house in a cool and most picturesque situation.

*** We are within a few yards of a fir forest, suggestive of Baden-Baden, and so advantageously posted that we can see nearly everything going on in the Bay, hear all the bugle-calls, and at the same time shut ourselves out completely from all the noise and racket of business and carriers' drays. *** We are within thirty minutes' walk of the barracks, and within a couple of stone's-throw of all the most admired and charming hill-side paths; so that it will be our own fault if we don't succeed in making ourselves comfortable, and getting some capital sketches of scenery hereabout.

Our house is a thoroughly old-fashioned Dutch house, thatched with reeds, with Flemish gable-ends, and a 'stoep', or terrace, like an Italian 'loggia'. It is neatly white-washed; the woodwork painted green outside, and all the rooms ceiled with teakwood, oiled, and varnished. The walls are at least fifteen feet high, and papered much in the same way as an English farmhouse would be. There are numerous out-offices for poultry, wood, horses, cows, &c., &c., and, in fact, we could easily set up an establishment at the rate of £1,000 per annum, and not be cramped for room. The plan of the house provides for thorough ventilation; and where we should place a mere passage, the colonial builders have put a voorhuis, – that is to say, a passage and room thrown into one, so as to make the dining-hall the coolest of chambers – full of teak cupboards built into the walls, and provided with at least four doors to gain access to different parts of the house. Of course, the windows are all delightfully old-fashioned, and you cannot pull down the upper ones because they are fixtures, and you cannot push up the lower ones because they open like casements, outwards. Instead of Venetian blinds, all the windows exposed to the sun have solid wooden shutters, so that the light can be completely excluded, and an afternoon nap enjoyed in the dark. As the floor is flagged with porous Dutch red tiles, the voorhuis would strongly remind you of many a picture of Flemish interiors; and I believe this sort of house is typical of farm-houses all over the Cape Colony.

Then we have a verandah of most primitive construction. It consists of a light framework of bamboos and fir spars, resting upon strong brick pillars about two feet square, and covered with the grass-green leaves of three or four varieties of grape vines. The vines look very old and very frail, but are twisted about horizontally on this open trellis work in huge snake-like coils, and, we are assured, will be crowded with big bunches of crystal and acorn and muscadel grapes by New Year's Day. At present they provide us with ample shade, and are a real luxury to readers out of doors. Much of my time is spent in the garden, which is not very big, but then it is very useful, being a mixture of kitchen and flower-garden, where cabbages and radishes are bordered by thyme and rosemary, and where myrtle and the prickly white roses are guardians of strawberries and lettuces. Of course, the flower-beds are full of stocks and pinks, lilies and dwarf roses, and all the old-fashioned list of floral friends; but you would be surprised to find the Cape gooseberry holding its own in *both* departments, and vieing with the tomato as a comestible and a wall flower. There is a very pretty little species of red tomato growing here, which is not much bigger than a pigeon's egg, and which makes a delicious and most delicate preserve; but I prefer the preserved *Cape* gooseberry to everything I have yet tasted, both for wholesomeness and for flavour. It is a curious, soft, flexible plant, like a monstrous petunia, with broad silky leaves, and an infinitude of straw-coloured gossamer pods, about as big as a green-gage, in which is enclosed an *orange*-coloured cherry, just as you would tie up a bonnet in a handkerchief. When quite ripe, they fall to the ground, and in a few days these pods are as finely reticulated as the most delicate Brussels lace, *veiling* the berry, in which condition they are brought to market, and sold for about a shilling a bucketful. Another favourite of mine is the 'nartjie', a dwarf orange, which is sold at our doors for six and eight a penny; and, provided you eat fruit in the morning only, no harm will come from the indulgence.

You should see our fine orange trees – at least twenty feet high, with leaves bright as a holly, and loaded with fruit in various stages of perfection – ripe at base, yellow in the middle, greenish-black at the summit, and powdered with blossoms everywhere. They are just lovely poems, most exquisitely expressed!

8th October.— There is only one drawback to our place of residence, and that is, that we have no shops, and the road up to it is rather steep; so we must either send into town for everything, or trust to the passing hucksters for fish, fruit, or vegetables. It has, however, had one good effect already, and has caused the forgetfulness of our servants to become their own instant punishment, for of course they have to make three or four trips where one might have done, and no Cape servant will walk more than he or she can help. *** Our neighbours here are very neighbourly, and spend most of their time either in their gardens or their kitchens, as sources of income; but then, poor things, many of them are very poor, though well descended, and genteel poverty all the world over must be hard to bear.

The sudden abolition of slavery must have been a dreadful blow to the real prosperity of the Cape; not so much from the fact of slaves being made free as from the *immediate* loss of services, that neither money nor love could replace in the labour market. I find, in conversation with all classes – who rather avoid the subject – that the misery inflicted upon the slaves themselves was very severe. Suddenly deprived of the superintendence of those who provided for their wants in every particular, the able-bodied went in for idleness, neglected their old, worn-out people who were past working for themselves, while the youngsters were left to teach themselves the handicrafts of which slave-owners had hitherto furnished and regulated the teaching. The consequence was, that the estates went to ruin, the slaves became paupers, the children grew up ignorant and careless, while the crowding and want of proper food soon reduced their numbers and strength. Money compensation could not bring other labourers in their place, and the absence of superintendence and regular task work soon worked out their own revenge upon thriftless loons.

One cannot walk down any of the beautiful long oak avenues abounding in our neighbourhood, or stroll for an hour in the narrow aisles of the extensive pine forests hugging the base of Lion's Head and Table Mountain, without seeing how much was done by slave labour, and how much has been thrown out of civilization by its sudden withdrawal. This question of coloured labour is so intimately connected with the poverty of farmers, the absence of specie, and the neglected condition of the splendid tracts of country, which might have been blooming like a garden had there been something more than the pressure of want to insure regular and industrious habits among the lower orders squatting and loafing in our midst, that one requires to be *on the spot* to see how practically injurious our warmest sympathies for freedom can become unless tempered by local knowledge and political insight into native character.

The curse of this country at present seems to be that the land is locked up in the hands of hereditary landlords, who, by the law of Dutch succession, and by subdivisions of landed property, have become the starving owners of broad acres, without any capital to develop the soil. In the opinion of clever, practical men, the Colony is full of good land; the country districts are full of able-bodied labourers; but the labour and the land cannot be brought together, because there is no coin to cement the union, and the labourer is literally not worthy of his hire. You will scarcely believe it, if I tell you that the women and children of a poor man's family, except in towns, are scarcely of any pecuniary help to him. The male labourers get a plot of land, in exchange for their toiling now and then; with rations and a few shillings during harvest time; but then the family earn next to nothing and spend their time in savage sloth. Of course, this statement is founded upon the knowledge of others, and I believe it to be correct. Yet the native seems to be a very good-tempered, easy-going, merry fellow, a gentleman at heart, not very clean in his habits, but gloriously lazy. His religion, his dress, his temper, his morals, are all equally free and easy; if he would only get fond of money, and take to trade, he would be readily managed; but then unfortunately, he will only work on compulsion, and spend every penny on pleasure or amusement. Were we in his place, probably we would do the same, as the climate is too pleasant to incite us to serious task-work; but what can we forecast of hinds, who, like the immortal 'Quashee', can live luxuriantly upon pumpkin, and calmly see cleared land revert to jungle and scrub?

11th October.— The more I see of this country, the more I am taken by the wonderful freemasonry that exists among all classes. Man-traps and spring-guns are all very well for free England, but the law of trespassing is apparently a dead letter out here, and you are at perfect liberty to ride or walk wherever you please, provided you do no mischief to property. No one appears to be surprised if you cross their grounds, or enter into frank conversation with their servants while at work; and I am always in a fidget with James, because he will persist in taking short cuts across enclosed fields, and exchanging the most abominable 'patois' with all sorts of people. He looks so good-humoured that I presume they think him incapable of being impertinent; and 'Sunbeam's' good looks and shining coat have carried us triumphantly out of a good many embarrassing positions, where nothing that we said could be understood, but where a handsome horse was sure to meet with ardent looks of admiration and approval from even wood-cutters and washer-women.

My own idea is that we are looked upon as slightly out of our minds; and certainly it does not smack very strongly of Belgravia to be prowling about the wash-places, and having familiar interviews with the good-tempered old souls, who are banging about our best linen sheets and gowns on the stones, and causing the buttons to fly off under stronger provocation than did dear old 'Peggotty's', when 'Barkus' informed her 'he was willing'. It is an amusing sight to stroll up towards 'Platteklip' in the afternoon, and there watch the hundreds of dusky damsels lathering and wringing, banging and pounding our unfortunate garments in the brooks that come leaping down from the Table Mountain. The bushes are covered for miles with snowy clothing; and these women are obliged to be up very early indeed in the morning to secure the best pools for washing, – walking sometimes nearly three miles up the stream; and, of course, they do not get home again till late. They are generally accompanied by their little ones, and by a tame goat, and pass the livelong day in the open air up to their knees in water. It must be very hard work, and yet you see them waddling down in Indian file with enormous bundles on their heads, their hands on hip, their faces hidden under their yielding burdens, but their tongues going at a merry pace. Occasionally, you will see the 'bambino', straddling his mother's hips, and fixed safely in position by a sheet passed round his fat little person, and tied across the parental breast, – the chubby legs sticking straight out, and the round woolly head wagging about from side to side like an animated knapsack – such funny round-eyed shiny little dots, in a constant state of unutterable surprise!

The extensive fir forests of Mr. Breda, of which I have already spoken, abut on to the Wash-place, and out of its broad fire-paths you see emerge small boys, staggering under enormous loads of firewood and brushwood, which they are allowed to carry away for a trifling sum. I don't exaggerate when I say that I daily see quite slips of wiry lads carrying upon their heads, loads of wood eight feet long, and as thick as a water cask. How they get such an enormous bundle upon their shoulders in the first instance would puzzle you. But the way they manage is this: they stand the load upright against a wall or tree; then taking a deep breath, these boys – probably not four feet high – plant their backs against the heap, grasp it firmly with both arms extended, and employing their hard heads as a fulcrum they tilt the whole mass forwards, and then stagger away swiftly with tottering feet for about two hundred yards – when they throw their loads down, and pause for ten minutes; and so on again as before. To see a train of these wood-crowned Atlases staggering down a hill is enough to frighten the quietest horse; but I suppose the boys gradually get accustomed to it; and whoever can carry away the biggest load, of course gets the most for his sixpence.

These lads are great bird-fanciers, and I have bought from them three or four varieties of Cape linnets that are capital singers. The Cape canary is yellowish green, and is an indefatigable singer, repeating his mellow notes by the hour together. Then there is a yellow-and-brown finch, called the 'Saasie', which runs up and down a limited scale with much sweetness and expression, but the singing is soft and subdued,

and, as it were, lisped out. The 'Pietje' and the 'Berg' canary are not unlike London sparrows in plumage, but they sing with great vigour, and are capital birds to put together in a large cage – especially if you have a good English canary to conduct the orchestra, when the row they make at break of day and at sunset is something deafening. Thus, you see, I am at my old trick of filling the house with noisy pets; and I love them the more, because I had always been given to understand that 'at the Cape the flowers had no scent and the birds had no song'; but this is certainly opposed to my experience. *** One of our friends has got quite a large aviary at the end of his 'stoep', and I assure you the collection of Cape birds is really surprising, both for plumage and noise.

I despair of giving you an intelligible idea of the land we are stopping in, unless you can realize fully the meaning of the statement, that, according to Herschel, the intensity of light at the Cape of Good Hope, compared with that of a *bright summer's* day in England is as 44° to 17°. Now, there is a health-giving influence in a bright atmosphere and a cloudless sky, which is not fully appreciated even by doctors, and I am sure it is one of the reasons why there is so little sickness at the Cape, in spite of the exposure. It is this that makes the rocks and peaks of Table Mountain appear as if they were suspended over our heads and exaggerates the real distances of objects in the landscape. Upon clear nights we can hear the goat-herds upon the heights above the Kloof-road folding their flocks, and calling out to each other; while the noise of the waves breaking upon the beach both at Camp's Bay and in Table Bay is as plain as if they were a quarter of a mile off, and yet they are really many miles distant, so dry is the air, and so transparent the atmosphere as an aid to both sound and sight. From where I am now writing, I can see cattle grazing near the Signal Hill, whisking their tails about, and snapping at the flies every now and then, and yet they must be at least two miles off. If I had used a telescope, it could not have made them out much clearer than did the naked eye. It is this seeming keenness of sight that gives such a charm to all our rides, as the prospect seems always boundless and full of detail. Whenever we reach some commanding position, the country stretches away in extensive plains, bounded by hills and sea; and there appears to be no limit to the liberty of the subject should you leave the beaten paths and roadways, and ramble hither and thither in search of the picturesque.

The view from the Crystal Palace Gallery and the country about Tunbridge Wells are not more charming to the eye than the prospect from our front door, or from the heathery wastes at the back of our house. The valley of Table Mountain is more richly cultivated than the vale of Gwynant, and the slopes of the Tigerberg, on the opposite side of Table Bay, are as smooth and as verdant as the Berkshire Downs, or our far-famed vale of the White Horse. What we look for in vain is the rich clumps of trees that lend such a charm to European scenery; and the Cape has no silvery streams to entice the angler to linger by their banks, or to enrich the soil by irrigation. You rarely meet sportsmen out here. Although the downs between Table Bay and False Bay are full of hares and wild rabbits now, where formerly prowled the lion and the jackal, yet the reeds and heaths are seldom bruised by aspiring Nimrods. James has certainly shot quail and partridges at the farms near Eerste River, but he always complains of the laziness of sporting-men out here, and I am not quite sure whether the smaller game is worth the powder and shot.

Monday, 14th October.— The cook has just looked in to know what I mean to have for dinner today, and this reminds me that you might like to be told something of the nature of the dishes of the country. In weather like this, nature loathes big smoking joints at table, and so I have been giving myself up to the *genius loci*. We dine now at one o'clock, and as the children and servants are hearty feeders, we are obliged to live largely upon vegetables and fruit. Instead of ringing the changes upon mutton and beef, roast, cold, and hashed, I have been taking lessons from our neighbours, as to the various modes of preparing colonial '*plats*', and I flatter myself that I have become a very competent 'chef-de-cuisine' by putting my nose into many a kitchen, and tasting everything that takes my fancy. Native cooks are rather too fond of greasy messes, by excessive use of sheeptail fat, but they are very clever in concocting savoury dishes out of very cheap and unpromising materials, and you may always look upon rice and onions as forming the chief ingredients for giving a relish to the poor man's food. With a few chillies, a pinch of salt, potherbs, and a little mutton, or snoek, or crawfish, or chicken for his curry, any cook will perform wonders. '*Babootie*' and '*frickadel*' and '*potatoe-pie*' are great improvements upon the minced meats of England; and '*sosaartjes*', '*smoor-picklaar*', and all sorts of vegetable '*breedies*' are importations from India, and much more savoury than devilled fowl, Irish stew, and ordinary side-dishes, in my opinion. Of course, you will smile at my taste – *de gustibus non est disputandum*; but then you know the proof of the pudding is in the eating, and I generally eat what agrees with me! Some of the salads are peculiar, but cooling. Lettuces, beet-root, cucumbers, radishes, or raw tomatoes, chopped up with hard-boiled eggs, dashed with vinegar and anchovy sauce, are quite elegant repasts, even at supper time; and I have medical authority for stating that stewed prunes, apricots, and peaches are decidedly conducive to health when eaten with venison, jugged hare, or the capital merino mutton of the Colony. Much of the beef here is bad, hard, and tasteless. Good juicy beef-steaks are seldom tasted out of England, but with poultry so cheap and abundant, the want of good beef is not much felt; and there are inexhaustibel supplies of fresh fish in the bays, to be sold at prices ridiculously low by the native hawkers.

You know my rage for preserves, and therefore will not be surprised at being told that I have been taking lessons in still-room mysteries that would set your mouth watering. Figs, melons, citrons, peaches, naartjes, tomatoes, loquats, gooseberry, blackberry, apricot, and hottentot fig, and a host of colonial acidities, have been duly stewed, boiled, and torturted into new forms of being by my inquisitive self. One dear old lady, Mrs. M—, who is exceedingly hospitable to the garrison, has even promised to show me how to brew liqueurs, and distil 'vanrhum' – the latter a most aromatic and powerful *elixir vitae*. If you promise to be very good and send me a regular supply of country gossip, perhaps I may yet send you some of it to warm your imagination and set your heart dancing! Had Mr. Pickwick ever tasted of this cordial, what revelations of convivial feeling might not have been the result!

Our supper time is generally at eight o'clock, light, varied, and not unlike a Scotch meat tea. At ten all are in bed. There is not much visiting at night. Dancing parties are going out of fashion. There are no theatres or concert-rooms – in fact, people live very quietly, and prefer to drop in upon their acquaintances between eleven and twelve, or between three and five p.m. After which hour they take their drive round the race-course, fanned by the sea-breeze, or else over the Camp Ground and out to Rondebosch. Walking long distances is not very fashionable. Equestrians like ourselves make long expeditions early in the morning, when the air is wonderfully fresh and exhilirating, and I could pass half my time in the saddle.

This is our great month for flowers, and the hills and commons are powdered with them. On either side of the main road to Simon's Town, within a mile of town, there are to be seen whole fields of white and purple striped butter-cups, deep orange masses of gorgeous wild marigolds, with gleaming acres of yellow sorrel, pink 'Africanders', and the most lovely Magenta coloured wild 'figs', blooming on sandhills just beyond the military lines. I have never seen anything to equal the metallic lustre of the 'everlasting' flowers, which are hawked about in great bunches by the broom-cutters for a few pence, and which, under the dryer's hands, are said to assume hues that add greatly to the rich designs traced out in camellia and silver-tree leaves by the young ladies here at Christmas and at Easter tide. Only yesterday, we ascended the neck of the Lion's Head by a steep zigzag woodland path, and walking along the spine of the hill on our way to the Signal-post, gathered every variety of bulb and heath, and delicate sparaxes, possible to conceive. I am afraid you will be getting tired of my raptures about the scenery of the Cape; but how can I help it? My heart is filled to bursting with the joyous freshness and purity of all the pictures about us in this land of clear, bright sky; and when the extensive view of the sea and far-spreading ocean bursts upon you from the crest of a hill that towers thousands of feet above them, the effect is very striking. Beneath you, the town with its thousands of flat-roofed houses lies spread out like a map, hemmed in by the lofty and almost perpendicular mountain walls. Around you beats and roars an enormous extent of water, wrinkled and crumpled up by the opposing forces of wind, rock and beach, and causing big ships to look like paper boats tossed about in a pond; while stretching away into infinitude of space and sky extend the filmy headlands and ranges of shadowy mountains that suggest but vaguely the resources of the interior and back country. As we gaze and gaze, the wind whistling shrilly over our heads through the cordage of the station – there floats up to our eyrie the clash and clang of sabbath bells, softened by distance. We see the crowds pouring along the streets on their way to numerous churches, and with many a slip and slithering slide we too hasten down the hill to thank our God for the many mercies He has vouchsafed us in the daily ordering and conduct of our lives. In moments like these, be sure our thoughts revert to the loved ones at home; in fancy, we join you in your walks and share in your conversation; and distance lends an extra charm to scenes, the memory of which stirs one's affections like a trumpet's blast, and awakens feelings which are too deep and too sweetly sad for tears.

CHAPTER FOUR

A grand excursion on Table Mountain

15th October, 1861

A propos of the Cape, I have just been reading the amusing journal of Lady Anne Barnard, kept while doing the honours of our Government-house under the Earl of Macartney in 1797–8; and I think you would be equally interested in it, were you to borrow it from Mudie's.

She is a bit of a 'quiz', and makes great fun out of the big feet and shapeless waists of the old Dutch 'vrouws' of that day; but while laughing at their fat, she is not forgetful of their good nature, and bears witness to their extreme kindness and hospitality – qualities certainly still flourishing in our midst. Though a great change must have come over the social life of the Cape since then yet I agree with her in thinking that a place in its infancy as to riches, conveniences, taste, and luxury, would not be mended by having amusements introduced that belong to a much further advanced period. What she wished in her time chiefly to effect was, if possible, to bring the nations together on terms of good will, and by having public reception days pretty often, to reconcile the Dutch to the sight of their masters, by the attraction of fiddles and French horns. If the fathers, who were lukewarm to the English Government, were sulky and stayed at home, the mothers and daughters always came; and '*to plough with the heifers*', writes Lady Anne, has always been reckoned a good mode of improving a reluctant soil. The good effects of this policy were clearly traceable to her tact and '*savoir faire*', and she must have thoroughly enjoyed bringing young people together – an advantage of which we are now for a season deprived, as our late Governor, Sir George Grey, has not yet been succeeded by another. Sixty years ago is a long time to look back upon; but the human heart is essentially the same everywhere; and were there more kindly, cultivated, and highly-bred people like Lady Anne in the world, we should not hear of so many silly women sighing for operas, theatres, gossip, and excitement, and sneering feebly at the want of 'ton', and dash, and style, in their more domestic but infinitely more usefully employed colonial sisters.

Some of our ladies here are so immensely supercilious, *** that I am not at all surprised that they sometimes get the cold shoulder in houses overflowing with sympathy and good nature. For ladies of this stamp, the Cape must be very dull indeed, and almost too hot to hold them, – with no balls, concerts, theatres, races, regattas, bazaars, and parks, &c., &c., &c., where to dawdle away the time, and display their smart clothes; – but only constant fine weather, lovely scenery, and unassuming neighbours, – no paupers, thieves, rebels, nor tax-gatherers – food cheap, servants civil, and no Court journal to follow – the sweetest liberty in everything – and wild flowers only too brilliant and beautiful to bloom beyond the day. And then the nights, so calm, so clear, so gloriously serene – stars trembling and shivering with radiant hues of light – planets like globes of parti-coloured fire studding the deep, deep violet blue of a cloudless sky – and on fine moonlight nights, the bright Diana riding calmly through the greenish heavens, chastening one's thoughts, paling the ineffectual fires of 'other worlds', and exerting a magician's sway over every tender spot in one's affections and memories. Oh! it makes me ill to hear pert subalterns' wives talking so sulkily and ungratefully of this Colony, when, in fact, their chief wants are more and more money to spend, and more or less of active practical good nature, to teach them *how* to spend it honestly. To see women of this stamp, who have perhaps never moved in Europe in other than third-rate middle-class society, turn up their chiselled noses at good-natured, and by no means vulgar Africanders, *because* their husbands or brothers are engaged in business, is one of the saddest proofs of insular pride and power of human conceit. One dear, real lady like our Camp's Bay hostess, or charming Mrs. C— with her bevy of handsome daughters, is worth, to my mind, dozens of these *blasé*, fallal, would-be-fine Corinthians: and I take precious good care not to conceal my opinion of them, when they take up my time, and bore me with their complaints and peevish details of petty annoyances. Let people only abstain from *vulgarity* and selfish indulgence in their own whims and caprices, and what on earth does it matter whether you had a grandfather or not to stand security for your 'genteel' manners?

I have been led into this train of unwonted ideas by some afternoon callers, who have thoroughly stirred up my bile, and provoked me to wrath, by sneering at our way of living, our hired house and its surroundings, in a tone of pity and of 'persiflage'. Such women would be unhappy, very unhappy, if isolated in Eden; but then, thank goodness, they are not likely to gain admittance there!

19th October.— The wind today is booming over our heads, and I have had a bad headache in consequence; so we have sent the children out to play in one of the oak avenues hereabout, and strolled out towards the scene of many a picnic, called the 'Verlaten Bosch', or the 'Deserted Lodge', not quite half a mile from this. Here you may enjoy solitude so complete, that you may fancy yourself far from the haunts of men. From the number of woods and avenues around this ruin, an invalid might enjoy a shady walk at all hours, even in the height of summer; and to you, who have seen the dark woods and deeper valleys of Baden-Baden, and the grounds about the 'Schloss', there will be no difficulty now in understanding why I express so much admiration for the best of Cape scenery; for the fir forests here would strongly remind you of the outskirts of the Black Forest, and recall many an incident of foreign travel. And yet, would you believe it, scarcely anybody seems to care for such haunts! All the sparkling water of Cape Town bubbles from tiny springs here collected, and there is an infinite variety of lovely ferns and mosses to attract the fairies hither.

The forests here are all the results of slave labour, if that could have been called slavery which was ruled by kindness, and flogged by the Fiscal's order, if it misconducted itself. Even Lady Anne Barnard speaks quite complacently of the purchase of slaves in her time, and a very good time the clever ones seem to have had of it – and now the steep sides and spurs of Table Mountain bear a monstrous crop of long lines of stone pines growing in regular rows about five feet apart, but shouldering each other as closely as a regiment drawn up on parade. As the wind sweeps over them, the dense green mass is stirred and gently swayed as with rolling fields of corn; while the creaking and groaning, crashing and smashing, of stem and bough–, rubbing acquaintance, and bowing and scraping to each other – are enough to exert a depressing influence on the spirits of the gayest party traversing their dry and well-littered avenues. Most of the trees are mere spars, very tall, very straight, decidedly top-heavy, and probably made lanky by overcrowding; but wherever space has been allowed them, they have expanded into very noble and picturesque trees, and are chiefly cut down for firewood. The further extensive planting of these fast-growing firs (it is generally admitted) would supply a defect of the country, as many fertile hills are very bare of trees, and from off the fallow grounds of farms, would improve the ragged proteas and dense rhenoster bush, now starving the soil. *** The smell of the sugar and buchu bushes, and the pungent odour of the bulbs and Africander lilies peeping out under their skirts, are the best cures I know of for a nervous headache! Can't you come and try them?

23rd October.— My notes today must be short, for we are all busy preparing for a grand excursion, and I am so excited that I can scarcely eat. *** Tomorrow we are thinking of ascending Table Mountain, as the day promises to be fine, and we have been having splendid moonlit nights for the last week. J— is going to join a shooting party to Constantia and Hout Bay, and we propose to get up a party of our own, to explore the top of the mountain, and compare experiences with Lady Barnard; and, if we can manage it, to walk over the hills to Constantia, and get our carriages to wait for us at a given rendezvous, so as to bring the ladies home again. This will test my strength – and we hope to see the sun rise, if not prevented by the sleepiness of some and the heavy hampers of others. I shall send you a full account of all we see, and hope it may prove worth the postage. Much will depend upon the day, and for personal equipment I shall certainly wear an old pair of boots, a light heart, and a strong pair of somebody's —s, for there is no knowing how many tumbles we may meet with!

Saturday, 26th October.— Ah me! how tired I am! Every bone in my body is aching with our tremendous journey of the day before yesterday; and yet what a glorious day it was, ever to be marked with a white stone, of which, by the way, there are myriads on the top of the mountain. To make a long story short, we clambered up from this side, and night found us at 'Belle Ombre', many miles distant on the other; but what a wilderness of rock, and what glorious views between! *** When the flash of the evening gun, always fired from the Castle, was followed by a clear, ringing report, repeated again and again by volley on volley of fitful echoes, now far, now near, rumbling, crashing, grumbling, and thundering among the rocky ravines and environs of Cape Town, J— said at once, we should have a splendid day for our excursion, and so it proved throughout. We therefore started off a note to Dr. H—, to tell him we were coming to his farm, and to ask him to be on the look-out for us in the afternoon, and sent off the guns and traps in the cart, to await our arrival.

To understand this narrative, I must tell you that our party was made up of Arthur P—, facetious Mr. G—, Mr. W—, Dr. P— and his wife, ourselves, and an artist friend – eight in all. They had a hearty supper at our house, after which, for fear of accidents, we made up rough beds for them all – and sent them to their rooms – prepared to turn out at one a.m., so as to avail ourselves of the light of the moon, then a little beyond the full.

It was quite a brilliant moonlight morning, as, preceded by three coolies carrying provisions, and waterproof rugs to keep us warm on the summit, we walked briskly through the suburbs. The streets and houses at that hour were weirdlike in their silence; every tree and object strongly defined in outline, but strangely altered by the moon-beams, – nothing stirring but the mounted patrols muffled in long dragoon cloaks, who challenged us gruffly, and the fresh air cold enough to bite your nose off.

In about an hour after starting, winding and twisting our way upwards, and ever upwards along a rough footpath leading to the 'Platteklip' (a broad, smooth ledge of granite, slippery as grease from the wearing of a little brook that glides like liquid silver over it), we ordered a halt, to rest a bit, take a 'soopie', and admire the calm beauty of the scene spread out before us. Here Dr. P— nearly came to grief by walking quite carelessly across the slippery slab – for in a minute it tripped up his heels, and sent him sprawling on his back. *** Meanwhile our coolies kept steadily at a slow, even pace, wriggling their way up among the loose round stones paving the dry gully which leads to the top, and we could hear them scrunching and rattling over the avalanche of water-worn pebbles far above our heads, long after we had lost sight of them in the gloom and deep shadows cast by the moon. Another 'soopie' was then served out, and we too prepared for the awful fatigue of following in their footsteps. Slipping back two feet for every yard we advance, we, too, dig our heels and long sticks into the shifty rolling stones, and slowly but wearily mount up an almost vertical track. Oh, how my chest did pant and heave, and how the muscles of my thighs seemed to stiffen, and grow numb from the steepness of the ascent; but I determined not to look back! At last we were all brought to a standstill by an enormous castellated rock which frowned down upon us poor puffing creatures, and barred any further apparent progress, until Mr. W—, who had been lagging behind, as an old stager guided us round it, and, lo and behold! there we were in a narrow funnel cleaving the mountain obliquely, and up which we all tottered, rather than raced, to see who should be the first to arrive. Be sure, I was not the last.

We were now three thousand five hundred feet up in the air, and a great deal too cold and shivery to do anything but dash at our rugs, and crowd round the big fires which the coolies had already made up for us. Wrapped in our waterproof blankets, we charged the gentlemen to run about and collect bush and heather, so as to keep the fires going, while we at once made some coffee, and enjoyed our bread and butter and 'biltong' like hungry school-boys. We soon, however, began to nod, till the morning gun announced the dawn; when creeping to the ledge of the mountain (while a substantial breakfast was preparing for us), J— and I peeped down cautiously over the dizzy precipice. This, I must tell you, is a rather hazardous undertaking, as the nerves of but few are strong enough to look down on the world below without growing faint and light-headed, with a yearning desire to throw yourself over. There was something so horribly fascinating in peering over the edge of this steep Cyclopian wall – looking down its rugged sides, and marking the jutting crags on which successively a body would fall in its downward flight, that you seemed powerless to restrain an almost irresistible longing to leap over, and dash yourself to pieces. Over five deaths are said to have been thus occasioned, as the results of imprudently placing confidence in one's strength of head; so I don't mind telling you, that I insisted upon J— holding me by the ankle, as I stretched myself out on my knees and elbows, ere venturing to use my eyes.

To see the sun rise from Table Mountain is perhaps not so fine a thing as from Monte Rosa or from Mont Blanc, but, for all that, it is very curious, and not half so dangerous. If you were to have heard all the laughing and joking that went on round the fire, while we were waiting for the sun to appear, you would have thought we had all been inhaling laughing gas. I never felt so exhilirating an atmosphere before, and Mr. G— kept us in roars of laughter by his witticisms and puns. *** Viewed from the entrance to the pass or 'Poort', Cape Town, with its right-angled streets and square 'blocks' of houses, looked like the ground plan of a very large building, dotted here and there with crawling snails – probably early market wagons. Table Bay was a gray expanse, like an oval sheet of zinc, speckled with ants and black beetles, and set in a frame of slaty coloured hills; and these again were all blended into one by the morning mists, out of which loomed distant peaks, with a background of cold steel sky glittering here and there with languishing planets and fading fixed stars.

Then gradually, as the morning wore on, little patches of cloud started into existence, and hovered like doves over a pale streak of primrose in the East. They had scarcely got ranged into line, when the pale and slender spokes of an immense but partially visible wheel of light radiated from the back of the Hottentots' Holland mountains, and warmed the heavens with their radiance. Long before the fiery axle could emerge, I noticed, how many of the sun's beams were partly obscured by thin clouds of pinkish dust, which slowly revolving, grouped into masses of snowy drapery, streaked with bands of soft colour. In a few minutes, like the scenery in a dissolving view, these masses faded into space, and then rearranged themselves into the most grotesque and fantastic forms, forming a canopy of the most gorgeous character. Simultaneously, the heavens were stained in every direction with rolling banks of clouds – pink, purple, saffron, pale green, carmine, and deep crimson – 'all mingled and commixt'. Word-painting cannot render justice to the reality. It was worthy of Turner's pencil – most superb!

At about 5 o'clock, the bright god signified his approach, by staining the highest crags with a rosy glow, and almost at the same instant his golden hair flared out from behind a broad peak. This to me was the most interesting moment of the whole spectacle, for as the blinding orb of day rose clear into view, the sunlight, travelling swiftly in a downward flight, in a flash, kissed everything in turn, and out of heavy inanimate lumps of forest and bush charmed a most beautiful landscape into active life. The face of nature, blushing, underwent a rapid metamorphosis. The crosses of the church steeples, the weathercocks, the skylights, and the attics of many houses blazed suddenly as if a shower of gold leaf had settled on the town. The sea, but a few seconds previously of a leaden aspect, now danced and glittered joyously; the mystery of the beetles and ants now resolved into ships and boats at anchor; the 'bulls-eyes' and stanchions and polished brass work of the shipping in the bay glowed like balls of fire, while the cotton sails of the fishing smacks and other small craft in the offing glanced brightly in the sunshine. The 'Blauw Bergen' and the high hills behind them assumed a *vivid cobalt* hue, and beyond these again, stretching away far into the interior of Africa, 'rank behind rank', ten distinct ranges of mountain and peak met our dazzled and wondering vision. Only a thin blue line of glancing surf – dashing on the beach like a bayonet charge – mapped out the coast, but the hoarse roar of the breakers was plainly audible from our elevated position, four miles off. The vibrations of the drums and bugles waking up the garrison also fell softly upon the ear.

As soon as the sun had climbed a little on his path, and the attendant clouds had lost their colour and faded away into space, we retired from our posts of observation, *raging with hunger*, and did ample justice to our strong coffee, biltong, 'carbonatjies', sausages, and hard-boiled eggs. Then many a song was sung and many a yarn was spun, under the influence of strong sunshine and the pure free breeze, while our friend the artist, painted away for dear life, so as to finish a capital view, and go back, as he came, with the coolies. After adding our autographs in white paint to the numbers already daubed over the rocks, we packed up the crockery, arranged some sandwiches, and decided to walk over to Constantia. Skirting the coping or rough edge of the flat but dampish table land, we strolled in light skirmishing order over to its most easterly end, whence, near the cairn of stones erected by Sir Thos. Maclear when measuring the arc of the meridian, we peered down on Rondebosch, Camp Ground, Newlands, Claremont, Wynberg, – all the richest scenery of the Cape district, now gay with patches of wild flowers, over a bare rocky wall, perpendicularly scarped for more than 2,000 feet. The abruptness of the descent of this side of the world-renowned mountain, and the number of huge fragments scattered at the foot, would almost seem to point to a most terrific landslip in days gone by. Immediately beneath us, snugly ensconced amid thick woods, and only to be detected by blue wreaths of smoke, lay villas, châteaux, and country retreats, with clearings and vineyards, and beyond these, out on the plains for about fifty miles, the 'Flakten' or Cape Downs – intersected by straight threads of red road and irregular strips of white sand, and having every 'vlei' and pool and footpath, farmhouse and hut mapped out on its brown and purple heather as vividly as on an ordnance chart – stretched away like an Indian carpet till lost in the misty fringes of Somerset West Strand and the *smoking* beaches of False Bay and Kalk Bay. And behind these again might be descried slopes, farms, and jagged purple heights, faded into thin air. To the extreme right nestled Wynberg, Protea, Diep River, Blue Lake, Muizenberg, Constantia, and the various native hamlets proper to every large estate; while the wide circle of the Atlantic was just visible like a silver zone clasping the rocky isthmus which would be an island, with Simon's Town at one end and Cape Town at the other, were it not for these sandy Flats shoaling up between the Bays.

Having taken our fill of the splendid and extensive prospect, we turned our faces to the south-east and set off on a tramp of discovery. Before us, jumbled confusedly together, lay immense rocks and rugged boles of sandstone, over and through which we had to skip and clamber, and force our way blindly. Track there was none. The morning breeze soughing through the reeds and flags, and whistling shrilly among the crevices of stones, cooled our foreheads and bade us step out briskly. Not a bird or living creature was to be seen, not even a baboon, but bulbs were numerous, mosses and bog plants abounded, and there were lots of immense gaudy blue, purple, and black-with-gold butterflies hovering over the wild geranium bushes. Nothing before us, nothing behind us, but a wilderness of rocks, grey with lichen, and varied with patches of stonecrop and yellow sorrel in the distance. Here and there we met with specimens of those freaks of nature, the curious orchids, and with gay groups of manyhued sparaxes and ixias, crassulas, disafloras, and the lovely 'Jersey lily', gleaming richly like *stained ruby glass*. Now if ever women earned their dinners that day, we ladies did. Mrs. P—, especially, was full of pluck and good humour, her jolly Irish face rather rosier than usual, and as for her boots, they were literally flayed. *** At one moment we were up to our ankles in moss, at another sliding over big rocks, then perhaps we would be brought suddenly to a standstill by a gaping chasm or an impracticable pool. Still we struggled on somehow, heedless of thirst and reckless of shoes.

The sun was now getting nearly vertical, when we resolved to halt for an hour under the inviting shade of two curious slabs of rock resting upon each other, and which Mr. W— (a perfect treasury of knowledge!) told us were nicknamed the 'Hen and Chickens', and which formed a pleasant shelter from the direct rays of the sun. At one end was a deep recess, and while we were finishing the remnants of our baskets, washed down by draughts of delicious cold water, Mr. W— entertained us with a graphic and flowery account of one of his many previous adventures on the mountains. Mind, you need not believe a word of it, unless you like.

'Some three years ago, when everything up here was as dry as tinder, and when bush fires were by no means uncommon all round, I was collecting bulbs hereabout with a German enthusiast in flowers, when we were suddenly overtaken by a fire on the mountain, and had to run for our lives, to this very place. Do you see that old stump of a tree yonder (pointing out a solitary tree) standing out like a gallows on the extreme verge of that ravine? Well, it was *just there* that we first caught sight of our real danger, little suspecting that the burning of the grass on one side of the hill could make us so thoroughly hot and uncomfortable on the other. All the morning we smelt smoke, but now we were doomed to taste the fire also.'

'Well, and what did you do?' laughed Mrs. P— . 'Did you run away?'

'Humph!' growled Mr. W— , drawing a long breath. 'Hearing the crackling of fire, I just took one look behind me, and there I saw a slender ribband of fire wind like a snake round the trunk of that self-same silver tree, and thrusting lithe tongues of flame through the leafy branches, leap triumphantly into the air, a very devil of a blaze! In a moment the grass at its foot, crackling and hissing beneath a wide shower of sparkles, suddenly flashed into flame and blazed like a train of powder. Fringed with a glowing hem, the smoke rose in dense columns, and scattering hot cinders before it, came whirling along at an awful rate right in our direction. Didn't we just then run, aye straight to these rocks! We reached this recess, cleared it of rubbish and then creeping in to the very back, pulled off our coats, plugged up the outlet, and soaking our handkerchiefs with brandy from our canteens, covered up our nostrils, and in an awful blue funk lay down to take our chance.'

'And were you not stifled? inquired J—. 'It must have been very hot, if the day was half so hot as this. Have a glass of beer, old man! It will refresh your memory.'

'My good fellow,' said W—, rather nettled, 'first let me finish my story. With a roar like that of a mighty bellows, on came the fire – gliding smoothly over rocks, snapping and crunching up dry twigs, scorching vegetation, and withering everything into ashes and dust. It just touched the stone you are sitting on – gobbled up the rubbish we had thrown out, and then with a loud whirr, and an angry grumble of disgust at not being able to get at us, swept off to pursue its ravages over the ground we had just been mooning over. Licking up the pools in its way, and baking the boggy spots, away it flew on its course of destruction, the reddened grass flaring into myriads of sparkles, – the ashes whitening the ground, and finally setting fire to the Camp's Bay side.'

'By Jove! what a lucky escape,' said Mr. G—, with a twinkle in his eye. 'How I envy you your powers of description. And did you really see all that you have told us, in a moment of fright?'

'Ah, you fellows may laugh,' retorted Mr. W—, 'but let me tell you there are worse dangers to be met with on this mountain than fire. Just you ask young P— there! Which is worse – fire or mist, my boy?'

'Oh mist, decidedly!' replied that modest youth. 'I was once up here with a picnic party, and brought my old Newfoundland dog up with me, to beat up the conies and fish out baboons. We had a jolly time of it knocking about, and strayed over to the end that overlooks the Devil's Peak, where poor young Carpenter lost his life. All of a sudden a black south-easter got up, chilling us all to the bone. Our shirts were saturated with wet, and in a few minutes we were all abroad in the thick fog, which hid us from each other, and made everything loom up like ghosts around us.'

'And how did you get out of it?' I asked.

'Well, fortunately one of us had a tiny toy compass attached to his watchchain, and knowing the wind to be south-east, we agreed to walk away to the left, *against the wind*, so as to keep off from the edge of the mountain. The wind howled so dismally that it was hard to hear one's voice, and so we stumbled on, till just as we thought we were half a mile from the "Poort", we heard my old dog close to us barking and howling in turns. Just then, there was a rent in the mist, and we caught a glimpse of the bay, and only fancy, we were within a few feet of the edge, when we thought ourselves so far off. The dog had sniffed the danger, and stopped to warn us. So we fired our guns off, and after shouting all together we were answered by our coolies who were cooking dinner not many dozens of yards distant, little thinking what a "shave" we had had of being served up cold, thousands of feet below.'

'But, surely, Mr. P—, you could not have walked straight to get so much out of your reckoning?'

'Oh yes, I did; but a black south-easter turns one's head, and probably we had all had too much breakfast that morning. But catch me up here again without a compass, it makes me quite shiver to think of it even now; so come, let us be moving.'

Getting again under way, we tramped on with renewed spirits till about four o'clock, amusing ourselves by hurling stones over the ridges to see where they tumbled, and watching the increasing enormity of their leaps, as each stone gathered impetus from every rebound, until at last they plunged far down into the ravines. We also came across the extraordinary parasitic plant called the 'old man's beard', – conferring a most venerable and hoary appearance on the boughs and gnarled stems of all the trees to which its long and tow-like fibrils were attached, – as well as the '*baviaan's touw*', or 'baboon ropes', – ascending and descending in cord-like ladders from many a monarch of the ravines. They would have made capital swings for thousands of monkeys had they been present.

At length, about six, the sun went down behind the dark lines of mountain and cloud, which in the west piled up 'an airy city, wall heaped on wall and battlement on battlement'. The valleys began to grow dim in the fading day, and the flowers of the night – or as they are called here the '*avond bloemetjes*', soon unfolded their tiny pearls and scented the air with exquisite fragrance. Guided by the fire-flies, which now emerged in myriads, we soon hit upon the Hout's Bay road, where we found Dr. H— had kindly sent on his own cart and ours to wait for us, and carry us off to 'Belle Ombre'. The drivers had been upon the look-out for us ever since three o'clock, and we were precious glad to rest ourselves on the comfortable cushions, and borrow slippers from his housekeeper before going to supper.

Our host was an oddity in his way, and had seen much and read more during his long residence in India. He had some capital pictures on his walls, one a copy of Guido's *Aurora*, and an equally clever cook in his kitchen, and I there for the first time tasted a most delicate fish, called the 'seventy-four' by some, and the 'Roman' by others, but which undoubtedly was as good as the best cod or turbot out of England. It is caught off Simon's Bay, and is much esteemed by epicures.

As our host was living '*en garcon*', – the ladies of our party elected to be conveyed back to town in our cart by young Mr. P—, while the gentlemen stayed over a few days for some shooting. It was a long drive back to town, and I was uncommonly glad to creep into bed by midnight. Be sure I did not awake till long after breakfast time.

CHAPTER FIVE

The howling nuisance of the South-Easter

10th November, 1861

We are now fairly in for two months of 'south-easters', and, from what I have seen of them lately, it gives one quite a new experience of the power of wind. During the past week we have been terribly flustered by this howling nuisance. It has been blowing great guns for several days together, lulling towards sunrise, and generally more furious towards sunset; but at intervals tearing over the town and bay in terrific gusts that are almost appalling from their force and fierceness. Sometimes the houses in town are quite obscured from view by clouds of fine red dust, while the waves of Table Bay are lashed and churned into galloping steeds, white with foam and scud, and as if impelled by the furies to sweep Robben Island out of their path. Around us the forest trees are in wild commotion, groaning and creaking dismally as the wind comes crashing down in a thick white wall, tearing away huge branches with ease. Although the air up here is cold and dry and not unpleasant out of doors, yet inside, oh! how close and stuffy are most of the rooms, for the sake of keeping out the dust. One pants and puffs for fresh air. Then you open the windows, and everything in the way of furniture is almost immediately disarranged. You fly to the garden, and, when there, can scarcely keep your eyes open for the irritating particles of dust. Your best flowers are shrivelled into straw; your prettiest plants look as if they had been burnt. In your neighbours' premises all is ruin, desolation, and waste. There is only one thing to do, and that is to get on to the Kloof Road where the wind has little or no effect, and then the change is delightful.

But it is the lull after the storm that really upsets one the most, making you feel languid, out of sorts, depressed, and indisposed to even think cheerfully; for then the wind has died away into a frizzling calm, succeeded by intense dry heat, and an almost hot-house atmosphere, enough to bake you brown. No wonder they call this wind 'the Cape Doctor', for no sooner has it left you than you have to put up with all sorts of disagreeable consequences. As for trying to do any shopping, it would be simply madness to attempt it. I tried it once, and never shall I forget the way in which I was twisted and twirled about until I was only too glad to take refuge in a cab. To venture into the streets, then, while a strong south-easter is blowing, is to expose yourself to ridicule and disgrace, for it is impossible to keep your balance, much less your bonnet, during its continuance. And then the clouds of dust, choking your windpipe and making you swallow the proverbial peck of dirt we are born to eat some time or other all in a minute or two; the rattling hail of small pebbles, and the frightful eddying blasts that toss your clothes over your head, wrench your shawl off your back, and pelt your face and eyes with a perfect battery of gravelly sand torn from the street surface, – are evils sufficient to make a Quaker lose his presence of mind. *** And all this time the Devil's table-cloth is being neatly and smoothly laid half-way down over the mountain, and a perfect cataract of wool and cotton is flaking off in big sheets and ragged bales of vapoury cloud, as if all the fleeces of the Colony had been suddenly sent flying over the summit, and tossed into space. *** And when, after two or three days' extravagance, the supply seems at length to have become perfectly exhausted, and the outline of the mountain is of grotesque and dazzling clearness, and its skyline appears to be only interrupted by funny groups of coolies or baboons sweeping away the fragments from the rocks, then the wind will occasionally blow with greater violence than before, even while the bright blue sky is perfectly free from cloud, and you might almost fancy yourself in Italy but for the wind.

Oh! but this wind is an awful infliction upon Cape Town residents. It is enough to make you cry to see the mischief done in one short night to the exposed flower beds of the Botanic Gardens – everything looking brown, withered and sapless, where two days previously all was green, crisp, and glistening with vigorous growth. The constant roaring in your ears is very irritating, and upsets your temper abominably. It makes your skin hot, harsh, and crackling; and my hair almost snaps and fizzes if furiously brushed during these trying times. *** Then we are sometimes blessed with a black south-easter, which is nothing less than a south-easter in the sulks, all tears, rage, and freezing ill-nature. The mountain is then quite buried in cloud, the air is laden with moisture, the winds run howling hither and thither, doors bang, windows rattle, horses jib, the rain descends, the dust ascends, everybody tumbles up against his neighbour, and no one knows whither he is going or where it will all end. Even the very pigeons are afraid to venture out, and pedestrians gaze very fixedly at their boots, while vainly trying to make headway against this oppressive tax upon locomotion.

Then, the dust – ah! my dear – you don't know what dust means till you have dwelt in Cape Town. To you, who are accustomed to have streets well swept, and the pavement kept clear of rubbish by constant relays of scavengers, how can you realize dust so fine that it works its way into your friend's drawing-rooms, defying sight, but spoiling piano keys, bronzing fenders, and toning down the too brilliant foliage of wall-papers into a very sober brown. Of course, there are water-carts; but, oh! so few and far between, that before they have well turned out of one dusty street the parched ground is as dry as if never soused at all. Then it is quite diverting to watch the lazy way in which the young imps who guide the quick-stepping horses, and sit-a-straddle of the hogsheads of wheels, go about their business of laying the street dust. With the check-string in the right hand, and the reins in the left, they keep jerk, jerking away, just sprinkling the streets, and making as few visits as possible to the troughs where they get their supply. Dirty salt water from the beach is often used, and leaves anything but a balmy odour behind; so that it is wonderful how people put up with the grievance. Were it not for the wind, however, the town would never get rid of one half of its abomination; so that we must take the good it does as a set-off to the mischief it works during the season, and be thankful for small mercies.

20th November.— The weather of late has been getting sensibly hotter; but I cannot say that I find it in any way to be disagreeable. Although the glass sometimes rises to eighty, there is very little of that sweltering sultry heat which we associate with an African summer. Provided you sit quiet, broiling in the sun is almost agreeable; and the labourers at noon think nothing of lying flat on their backs, drawing their hats over their faces, and going fast asleep in a blaze of sunshine. In fact, our life out here would be very hum-drum indeed if we did not spend so much time out of doors. Gardening means personal exertion; and I know one old gentleman whose chief exercise is to get up early in the morning before the dew is off the grass, and mow all his lawns smooth with his own clear-sweeping scythe; while many ladies would never have gardens at all if they did not do all their potting and transplanting with their own hands. This open-air life has already robbed me of gloves and parasol; and I think one's moral cuticle seems to grow thicker also in this sensuous climate. It is not that I have grown stronger-minded, but I fancy familiarity with colonial surroundings has made me less sensitive to social requirements, and more content to 'take the goods the gods provide us'.

Barring the wind, I find my life here very endurable, and you are quite mistaken in conjuring up the host of evils contained in your last. Of course, if the heat should grow intolerable, as we may probably expect at the time when you are shivering over your Christmas fires, why we must only adjourn elsewhere, and cultivate the Muses in shade. There are lots of places from which to choose.

Our *suburbs*, such as Wynberg and Rondebosch, on the other side of the mountain, are said to be deliciously cool and free from wind, and very much resorted to by those who can at all afford the luxury.

Were it not for the children, it would be delightful to make a round of visits to many pleasant places situate on the other side of Table Mountain; but it is such a tax upon our friends' good-nature to be dragging the family about with us, that hitherto I have forborne from accepting invitations. *** There is one place, however, mentioned by Lady Anne Barnard, called 'Paradise', which amply justifies all her praises; and in its immediate neighbourhood the Viceroy is wont to take up his summer residence; although, for my part, I infinitely prefer the house and splendid adjoining estate of 'Grootschuur', now in the possession of the Hon.—. 'Westbrook' has a fine view over the Flats; but 'Grootschuur' is a truly princely residence, and is almost buried in trees, extending right up to the foot of the mountain. Among them are groves of the lovely silver pine, and magnificent specimens of colonial oak and fir, growing to an *enormous* height. The owner of this place is a rare specimen of the old Dutch school, and nothing could exceed his kindness and hospitable courtesies during our too brief visit. He pointed out to us with great pride the boundaries of his estate, said he looked upon his trees as he would have looked upon his children had he been blessed with any, and that he never allowed any to be cut down unless they showed signs of decay or were injured by storms. If every land-owner were as conservative as this polite old gentleman, the chief drawback of the country would rapidly be got rid of. I suppose there must be thousands of young trees on this huge slice of land, and yet they never think of thinning them out.

If, however, you wish to see a pleasant sight in the way of silver trees, you should join us in a ride to Bishop's Court, over what is very properly styled 'Silver-tree Hill', by a path leading from Wynberg, where our troops are now established in a 'Sanatorium'. Such grand scenery is literally thrown away upon the residents and the soldiers in camp, who think more of coolness than intellectual luxuries, and laugh at the idea of climbing a steep hill to see a sun-set; but the Bishop and his family are immensely proud of the well-wooded valley in which they have secluded themselves from the world, and in this calm retreat can almost realize the happy dream of Rasselas, so full of beauties is the surrounding scenery. The Bishop has a bright sparkling, sherry-coloured river skirting his property; and along the banks of it are to be seen as pretty little '*bits*' as ever were sketched from the pools of the Conway or the Wye. *** I suppose it is rather wet at

Protea in winter, for — told us that the water-falls above their property are upon so grand a scale that when full they can be plainly seen and heard two miles off; and that they cause the Liesbeek to sometimes rise six or seven feet in a single night. They showed us a primitive bridge, self-constructed by the river burrowing away at the roots of an immense poplar, until it tumbled across the brook, the banks of which were here at least sixteen feet high, and I can quite fancy the roaring and whirling of the flood when in full spate.

The bed of the stream was full of big, smooth boulders, evidently swept down from above; and the crumbling walls seemed to be packed full of myriads of French rolls and crusty loaves of *petrified* bread. The fantastic creepers, twining their strong tendrils round the ragged roots of the overhanging trees, served to bind the mould somewhat; while the yams, pig-lilies, and brilliantly-green varieties of fern flourishing on every ledge, gave an animation to the scene worthy of Birket Foster. These poplar trees shoot up to a considerable height, and at the slightest breath of wind their quivering leaves shimmer and rustle like the veriest aspens; and as there is always a gentle murmuring issuing from the brook, you can fancy how soothing is the blending of these sounds on a thoroughly sunshiny day. For those who like to climb a bit, the panorama spread out before you, when standing upon the hill overlooking Bishop's Court, is really marvellous for variety; and though I admired our extensive view from the top of Table Mountain, I liked the scenery here even better when seen at closer quarters. The presence of the steep massive wall of mountain as a background has a most impressive effect, and the numbers of fine trees growing about the ravines and spurs make the landscape full of interest. Of course, flowers were everywhere, and the number and variety of native heaths are very distracting and beautiful. They abound upon the hills as well as upon the Flats, and can be gathered in quantities right up to Wynberg, which, as all the world knows, is one of the prettiest villages in the Colony, and on the direct road to Constantia.

The ride home through Claremont and Rondebosch is very charming. The old fellows who planned it, and the wealthy burghers who planted the roadside with wide-spreading oak trees, and filled their gardens with rare exotics and lustrous shrubs, richly deserve the praise which all must shower down upon their memories who are tempted to pass that way in the dog-days. It is like a triumphal procession, culminating in a hill, about three miles from town, called Mowbray, looking from the top of which you might fancy yourself on the road from Tunbridge Wells to Tunbridge, so wide is the prospect, so fair the scene, and all so thoroughly English.

From the top of this same hill there is a splendid side view of my favourite Devils' Peak, and a range of mountains trending to Simon's Town. The land between it and the main road is as finely cultivated as it would be in England, and it gives one quite a thrill to witness such thorough *high* farming so far from home. Overlooking it on a bluff, is a 'blockhouse' in ruins, about which, no doubt, some story must be attached, as I suppose these were placed there for offensive as well as defensive purposes before the Cape passed into our possession. Be this as it may, it has a most picturesque effect, and tells capitally in the middle distance. I wish I could send you a good sketch of it, and the grand old mountain behind.

28th November.— Our visit to Bishop's Court reminds me that I have never yet complied with your wishes about the churches and the clergy here. The fact is, we ought always to attend the Military Church, but don't, on account of the distance, preferring the so-called Cathedral of St. George's, where everything is hideously plain, and the intoning almost too tedious for any but saints; but the preacher is very eloquent and earnest. The church itself is a huge whitewashed barn, with a tower like a succession of blacking bottles standing on each other's shoulders in regular acrobatic style. Beyond a few mural tablets, there has been no attempt at decoration, no stained glass, groined roof, or any of the usual architectural accessories of a place of worship. It is just a big square building, and can hold a large congregation, and it is high time the Protestants here did something to improve its shabbiness. The Dean is a hardworking man, and is always on the trot; but the clergy here don't mix much in general society, and if you want to cultivate them, you must join them in their rounds among the poor. The life they lead in the poorer districts is very fatiguing, and how they get through to much work is surprising. *** District visiting among the ladies must be almost impossible here, but there are many other ways of proving your benevolence, especially by helping to get up bazaars, teaching in Sunday schools, &c., and though last, not least, supporting the local charities. The population of 30,000 is too mixed to make it safe for ladies to go about quite unattended; and one's motives are liable to misconstruction by the ignorant many; but there must be a wide field here for missionary enterprise. One thing is curious, and that is, the numbers of children of all creeds who attend the infant schools, without apparent offence to their parents' view of religion. These little chits have capital voices, and sing away *con amore*, while learning by rote. Ragged schools here are fully of precocious little monkeys, and their faces and eyes are bright with intelligence. The answers you get from them beat anything you ever yet saw made fun of in *Punch*; and I am quite sure that the average Cape 'boy' is quite equal in sharpness to the '*gamin*' of Paris. Whether he will improve as he grows older is quite another thing; but if I may judge from what I have heard and read in the Cape papers about the wretched homes of the poor, I should fancy not. According to eye-witnesses, some of the dens visited by our clergy are mere cellars – gloomy dungeons, where during the day candles have to be lit, because there had been no provision made for sunlight entering, except through the doorway.

This I hear is another relic of the old slave times, and I have had the curiosity to go into one or two dismal dens, the poverty and unwholesomeness of which fairly frightened me out again. How is it possible to maintain life, much less health, in such airless vaults, and drag out existence on old rags, and offal? Yet the thing is done, and no one seems to think it at all worth inquiring into. No wonder small-pox epidemics have so frequently attacked the coloured people. These dens are just the places to breed them.

The public buildings here are in what you may call the 'packing case' style, and must be anything but luxurious. If they are half as dingy inside as they are dirty and weather-worn outside, they must be indeed happy hunting grounds. The Post Office, especially, is a sight to see. Some of the houses here have some queer ornaments stuck on to their parapets and corners, usually seated figures, griffins, cherubs, lions, &c., &c., and the ordinary sweepings of stone masons' yards. Nothing can well be imagined more comical than to look at the battered brick-and-plaster images of lions couchant on the gates of the South African College. They have been mended from time to time by native masons, till all fierceness has left them, and they look in a chronic state of wanting poultices to reduce swellings in odd places, and relieve the mumps; you cannot conceive how funny it makes them look.

Perhaps the most remarkable building here is the range of barracks, constructed by the Dutch East India Company. The walls are at least four feet thick, and all built out of small Dutch bricks brought out direct from Holland. These bricks are as hard as flint, and cannot now be procured; but the barracks must have consumed millions of them. Another trace of Dutch rule has been wiped out of the town by the filling up of the system of open canals, and their conversion into hollow streets, the drainage being carried off by brick tunnels to the sea. Men are divided here as to whether the new plan is half as good as the old for a hot town. Time will tell.

Some of the relics of old times, I am told, are still religiously kept up in the more remote country town, and it is very diverting to hear old-fashioned people hold forth on the quaint ideas of the days when they were young; when young people were kept in their proper places, and when Government settled everything for you, from the clothes you wore, to the dishes you were allowed to put upon your table. I expect the 'niggers' in those days had sharper mistresses to look after them than we now see; and that the class of servants then bred here were less independent and better trained to their duties. At all events, they seem to have been made to turn their hands to anything, and could safely be trusted then to do what now neither money nor love can procure. I hear funny stories descriptive of sumptuary laws, of modes of conducting funerals, of the relations of children to parents; all of which, I presume, are now considered obsolete and in bad taste. And so the world wags on, 'always mending, never ending, always grumbling and offending'.

4th December.— By the merest accident I learned today that our old washerwoman's daughter, Rachel, was going to get married to a young Malay tailor; so I had the curiosity to get invited to the proceedings, as I greatly wished to inform myself on the matter. At the appointed hour one of our maid servants set off with me, not to the bride's house, but to that of the mother of the bridegroom, where in great state and clad in gorgeous array sat enthroned the heroine of the week. Early that morning she had been carefully fetched from her mother's house by the bridegroom, followed by relatives and bridesmaids, and then duly installed in the midst of her maidens. This is the first stage. Having presented her future husband with a beautifully-embroidered pocket handkerchief, he then departs in the company of a priest to the Mosque where the marriage service is to be gone through. The bridegroom is now directed to put his right thumb upon the priest's, who thereupon immediately covers their joined hands with the bride's gift, makes him plight his troth, and after considerable chanting and reading from the Koran, finally pats him thrice upon the head with the sacred volume, and the ceremony so far is completed. These two then return to the house, where festivities are going on, and where the happy couple, together with their friends and such of the public as like to look in, spend the rest of the day in dancing, singing, and feasting till sundown, when the bride and her attendants are again escorted back to her mother's house.

This sort of thing will go on for seven consecutive days, at the end of which time – the matter will have been so thoroughly published – that Mrs. Samodien can then in peace set up her own house and consider herself a wife. On each of these seven days, the poor bride is expected to appear in a different dress, each one if possible more gorgeous than the last, and sit for many tiresome hours to be stared at by all comers. We were much surprised by the warm welcome we received, for the hostess, a fat jolly-looking old Malay, as clean as a new pin, stiff with pride and rustling with highly starched petticoats, and with her smooth black bands skewered up tight with two gold bodkins, and shining with cocoanut oil, at once came to the front, and with a broad smile of welcome ushered us into the 'Salle du Ceremonié', where we were introduced to the young olive, and almost pretty bride as *'een van die officiers' juffrouws van de Kasteel'*. Blushing through her pale brown skin, the poor girl tried to rise up and receive us, but was so incommoded by all her finery, tight white satin boots, &c., &c., that she quickly sank back again in her satin-covered arm chair, which was wreathed with gold and silver-gilt leaves, and seemed a fit resting place for her richly draped figure. Her costume was really almost elegant. It consisted of a white satin skirt, with any amount of richly embroidered slips beneath, artistically revealed by a slight looping up of the dress in front as if by accident. The loose Garibaldi body which all Malays wear was on this occasion composed of the finest gauze and lace, whilst the raven black hair was arranged in many shining plaits, with a wreath of gilt leaves and orange blossoms surmounting the whole. Of course white gloves and white satin boots gave a finish to the stylish *toutensemble*. Need I say there were *no cards, and no veil*!

Having looked as long as I decently could, without utter rudeness, and spoken a few kind words of approval, I was taken into a second chamber, where, as a guest to be honoured, I was permitted to inspect its arrangements. It was the bride's bed-chamber; and the dressing-table, mirrors, washing-stand, &c., were tricked out with gold and silver wreaths, and even the floor was strewn with scraps of foil and artificial flowers, regardless of expense. To do things in this fashion must exhaust all the savings of the family, but *chacun à son gout.* Thinking we had intruded quite long enough upon these civil people, we were just going when they insisted upon my taking some refreshment before leaving. So as I thought acceptance would oblige them I stayed, and was led into a *third* room, where every description of pastry and sweetmeats were displayed on a long table for the benefit of visitors and friends, and really everything was beautifully arranged. We departed quite pleased with our visit, but not envying the poor bride the wearisome ordeal of six days of feasting and celebrations, through which she would have yet to pass before being allowed to retire quietly into domestic life again. Only fancy what a trial of patience it must be to have merely to *sit still*, and allow yourself to be criticized for a week. No wonder a Malay woman seldom gets married *twice*, though Malay husbands frequently marry a couple of wives, when able to afford the luxury.

CHAPTER SIX

Christmas festivities at Wynberg and Newlands

16th December, 1861

It is really getting almost too hot to write! and the children are now so troublesome and fretful with the heat, that I am greatly disposed to carry out James's suggestion, that every nursery should have a deep well attached to it, in which to suspend in baskets all fractious youngsters – so at once to cool and to quiet them. As it is, I have begun to act upon the plan, invented by the Dean's wife, of putting them regularly to bed at noon, so as to give them a chance of sleeping till three or four. This will bleach them, no doubt, poor things, but it will at all events save them from slow starvation, as they will scarcely touch anything but fruit now; and the doctors say that the fruit season kills more young children than the wet winds or excessive heat. The Dutch, I must tell you, rise so early that a twelve o'clock dinner is honestly earned after seven hours dawdling about, and then they have a long 'siesta' in their darkened rooms: after which coffee and cakes, tea and '*comfáát*', until it is time to go to bed again at ten, so that evidently English habits must now learn to give way to Colonial Dutch. *** After a particularly warm day, when the slightest exertion makes you hot and 'stickey' – it is very enjoyable sitting out under the verandah, and inhaling the delicious cool atmosphere of the glorious evenings. Then, when the moon is brightly shining, you can read your book, and even newspapers by its light, and on still starlight nights, when Sirius and Jupiter are sufficiently large and bright to glint their glittering rays on the sea; and when the dazzling Southern Cross is blazing with its constellations and 'pointers', as I have never seen stars blaze elsewhere, you can place a naked candle on a table and read in the open air, undisturbed by any flickering of the flame, or anything more unpleasant than a moth. These pure, clear nights are simply *heavenly*; and if I was not afraid of the cold and dew, I could almost make up my mind to sleep out on the stoep.

In the way of interesting sights, you cannot conceive what a fine thing it is to witness a thunderstorm breaking upon Table Mountain, *at night*. Of course, there is a terrible cannonading, – but the flashes of lightning give such lurid glimpses of towering peaks, and steel-gray rocks – the thunder-clouds keep rolling on so steadily like advancing waves of angry lions – while the echoing ravines and caves reverberate with sound, that on all sides hell seems to gape, and darkness grow deeper, at every successive crash. One of our servants comes from St. Helena, and the effect of peals of thunder upon this poor lad's nerves for the first time was almost ludicrous from his abject terror, and very evident inexperience of such heavy artillery practice in his own island home. Up in Natal, where thunderstorms are *very* frequent, scarcely a summer day passes, without some noisy interruption of this kind to the noon-day sleepers; but then the soil is full of iron-stone, and the heat there, I am told, is something tropical and frightful.

Another curious effect of the heat is the mirage on Robben Island, and the coast opposite us. Here, in broad daylight, you will be deluded by seeing the island lifted higher and higher out of the sea, until it suddenly parts like a stranded ship, and floats away into the oddest shapes; quite small bushes above high-water mark are magnified into enormous giants of the forest; wastes of white sand dance in the sunshine like rippling swift-flowing rivers, –while a few sparrows taking a sand-bath in the beach-road at Green Point, will suddenly turn into long-legged herons, stalking about solemnly in blue shallows and swallowing fish. Then perhaps, on top of this, there will come a sudden fall of the thermometer, and in a very short space of time, out of the sea, a tremendous fog-bank will come sweeping down with broad white wings round the town, until everything is clasped in a chilling circle, which sets me coughing, and provokes sore throats. Yet, wonderful to relate, in spite of all these changes, there is but little sickness here.

Apropos of fogs – only yesterday morning I beheld a very curious sight. As we were returning from an early ride round the Kloof, there was a thin mist brooding over Table Bay, which effectually converted all the hills and peaks above a certain horizontal line into a number of detached islands; but as the sun increased in power, the line of white sea gradually ebbed lower and lower, until at last the real beach came into view; and the upheaval theories of geologists were strikingly reduced to practice.

26th December.— Thank goodness – the last few days have been cool! Our Christmas day was not a very lively one, as colonists regard it religiously, and reserve all their merriment and romping for the New Year, just as we do in Scotland. The cathedral was very nicely decorated with wreaths of silver leaves, japonicas, pomegranate blossoms, and stained everlasting flowers, and the effect of the scarlet upon grey and green was very pretty. In the afternoon I looked in upon the Dutch Reformed Church, which boasts a dome of enormous span, resting simply on the four walls, without any central support whatever; but beyond this, the building and the service are equally plain and unattractive. The church bells were clanging furiously the greater part of the day, and altogether the scene was as thoroughly Scotch as the strictest Sabbatarian could have desired. At the same time, I have no doubt but that people were also quietly enjoying themselves in various nooks and corners and partaking of champagne and bottled stout, with fruit galore. Wine and dessert are so very cheap and varied here, that he must be a very poor creature indeed who cannot now provide himself and friends with figs, peaches, plums, apricots, strawberries, walnuts, and raisins, to be washed down with 'hanepoot', pontac, frontignac, or sweet Constantia ports and sherries, at something less than two pence a glass! Within a few weeks more we shall have abundance of grapes and watermelons – with bananas and pineapples grown at Natal – and cherries perhaps from the Cold Bokkeveld, so that picnics may then readily become the order of the week, and all idea of labour be thrown to the winds.

Here, as elsewhere, people are kinder than ever at Christmas time, and I am sure if I could only accept one quarter of the engagements offered us, I should be well occupied for the next three weeks in enjoying Cape hospitality. There is something very catching in the off-hand way in which friends put themselves at your service, and if I stop much longer in this country, I suspect I shall find myself one fine day inviting the whole garrison to a perpetual round of feasts at my expense. When you consider that everybody keeps horses – that the price of wine, of forage, servants' wages, and the many etceteras of housekeeping are exceedingly cheap, it really costs comparatively little to entertain. Much that wealth can give in England can be procured here at a very reasonable expense, but I am afraid that it is not so easy here to amass fortunes and earn large incomes. Good wine costs less than one shilling, but then the shilling is very slow in coming. The keep of a horse rarely exceeds £2 a month. Grooms are well paid at £2 to £3, and made to look after three horses if necessary. If the people were more energetic and industrious, I think the Cape Colony would soon become very thriving; but the apathy of all classes, *both high and low*, is simply astounding. The women and children do literally nothing. The men just potter about *pretending* to work, and by one day's wage of half a crown can live upon snoek and rice for a week. There are no settled trades nor regular industries. From year's end to year's end they all just eke out their lives, neither toiling in sun or shade, and only spinning out yarns about the hardness of the times. Why, if the Cape could be bodily exchanged for Ireland, what a change would not soon come over it by the mere introduction of British blood and brains with capital. As a friend of mine quaintly observed last night: 'Nothing but a severe frost every now and then is wanted to make the Cape prosperous, for it is impossible to make people lay up against a rainy day or an old age of want, when want and rain are such perfect strangers to them'. In the mean time, it is a very great pity that they are so lazy and wanting in enterprise, as they are as easily pleased as poor Paddy, and very good-natured, and seem to know how to spend their money like gentlemen.

Wynberg, 4th January, 1862.— The intolerable heat – 80° in my bedroom – has at last sent us here. It is a very pretty place, but *shamefully* neglected. Everything seems tainted with decay; and yet there are few villages in England to compare with it, for natural beauty of position and surroundings. Not very long ago, this was the favourite haunt of Indian officers, and when full of dashing equipages and stylish turn-outs must have been a lively place of residence. At present all the nice cottages are tumbling to pieces; the gardens are choked with weeds and brushwood; the roads and bridle-paths are worn down to their foundations; and melancholy may be said to have claimed Wynberg for its own. Beyond a couple of wretched old boxes on wheels called omnibuses, and a dozen or so of overworked horses grazing upon the extensive commonage, there is little to remind one here of either the road or the turf. And yet the influx of twenty families, of moderate fixed incomes, would soon convert this charmingly laid-out village into something very prepossessing. The orchards and gardens only want a little more looking after to make them full of fruit and flowers; and the trimming of the hedgerows and the shady avenues, and a general tidying up of the streets and watercourses would soon put quite a new life into the old place. The queer old tumble-down cottage of eight low rooms, in which we have now gone to burrow, is hidden away in a fir plantation; and if you were not supplied with a clue, would be very difficult to find on a cloudy day. We have long narrow avenues extending in every direction, and I almost defy the sun to touch us with a freckle. Here we let the children race up and down the whole day; and though the thatch is very ragged and mangy, and half the glasses are wanting in the windows, yet a couple of tradesmen will soon alter the aspect of things, and I mean to give a *fête champetre* every week, so soon as the pump can be got in working order, and the well cleared of its rubbish. Here in a perfect wilderness we mean to work like Trojans in making ourselves comfortable, and astonish the natives by an exhibition of English energy, in cutting down trees, ripping up weeds, and making this cottage in a wood one of the wonders of our small world.

18th January.— We have been here just a fortnight, and oh, what fun it has been to receive visitors and explain our plan of action to them! 'And did your husband *really* dig up the whole of that field? and did you *really* put up those curtains yourself? and do you *really* mean to have a flower garden here? and so forth, are questions constantly dinned into our ears, until I sometimes fancy I must have outraged all the proprieties, by trying to realize the life of a backwoodsman, but – bids me work on steadily, saying, 'The life is low, but so is the rent, and what on earth does it matter, so long as it keeps us in health?'

Our pomegranate hedges look very pretty indeed now they are clipped a little. The bright scarlet flowers contrast nicely with the dark green foliage and make them no bad substitute artistically for holly. The thicket of quinces has been well hacked about and most of the neglected creepers are set running again upon fresh supports. All the rose trees have been pruned, and in a short time we shall look quite gay. The fences of prickly pear too are thronged with bright yellow flowers, and woe to the unfortunate wretch who tries to force his way through their thorny shields, to steal our pumpkins.

And what about our neighbours? Well, we have some rough diamonds near us, especially an Irish surgeon, whom we called in to extract a tooth from our cook, but who made us laugh so immoderately at his original mode of proceeding – kneeling on the floor – that he broke his key as well as her molars, and then wished to be paid for the *double* injury! A true son of Erin is poor Dr.—, but you never heard a man tell a story so badly, or take so long in the telling as he did. He hummed and he hawed, stumbled and rambled to such an extent that it was a wonder, like the old woman's pig 'he ever got home that night'.

His competitor in the village is a wonderful specimen of the old school – courtly, urbane, and full of old world politeness. I heard he was nearly eighty years old, and had fought at Trafalgar with Nelson, and must in his youth have been a remarkable man, and yet – will you believe it? – this white-headed old gentleman came to see us in his carriage, wearing thin patent leather boots, and jaunty well-cut trowsers, strapped down tightly over them, and bearing his years as if he were in his second youth, instead of close upon his second childhood. Of course, he was full of village gossip, and promises to be a most valuable acquaintance; but what a fate, to be picking up crowns at his time of life! It shows what a healthy place this must be.

22nd January.— There is no doubt about it, but that Wynberg is very quiet, not to say dull. After the various omnibuses have started off with their male cargoes in the morning, the village is very deserted till five o'clock, when the husbands return again; but as the sun sets here sooner than it does in Cape Town, there is always an hour or two of comparative twilight, during which people ramble about a good deal. Like most hill villages – Wynberg is made up of straggling groups of houses with large gardens and verandahs, dotted about everywhere over a richly wooded area of nearly a mile, and in guidebook fashion, it might fairly be described as the connecting link between the garrison and the Naval station at Simon's Town, largely producing fruit, flowers, and babies in great variety; with its local industries confined to crochet, knitting, and mild tea-table gossip. The chief trade is in vegetables, fish, and roadside hostelries; and one or two general dealers are enough to meet all demands.

The great glory of Wynberg is its shady avenues. These extend in every direction, and are delightfully planned for horse exercise; and as the country all around is cut up with sandy paths, leading, however circuitously, to some pretty vineyard, château, or farm, you have only to keep cantering on to ensure a fine view sooner or later. We make up riding parties, and scour the hill sides and flats, away over the Black River, to Kirstenbosch, Constantia, Kalk Bay, and even as far as Blueberg sands. With a fine cool sea-breeze blowing in your face, with your horses dancing like canoes under you, and a wide prospect to be had for the trouble of putting on your habit, can you be surprised if we enjoy our life here amazingly? I am getting quite fat upon all this exercise, and acquiring quite a colour again; and as soon as I can muster up courage to look a photographer in the face, I must send you a portrait of myself and 'Sunbeam' to bear practical evidence upon this point.

Grapes just now are coming into season, and so are watermelons, and you would be surprised at the cheapness of fruit. Fancy getting six to eight large bunches for sixpence; melons, according to size, range from three pence upwards; and the luscious green and brown figs, at four a penny, are bigger than a baby's fist, and are as cold as ice when eaten early in the morning. The whole day long we are munching fruit; and the roadside groups of natives feeding *al fresco* are just like transcripts from Murillo's pictures. What with cheap fish and cheap fruit, I could give you a capital family breakfast for less than a shilling, and, I need scarcely add, there is always enough for one's friends besides.

24th January.— The best of Wynberg is that it is so centrally situated. Whenever Simon's Town Dockyard is joined to Cape Town by telegraph and railway, Wynberg will certainly grow into a large town, as it is the centre of the best wine districts, and admirably convenient for both soldiers and sailors. The present tenants are not a very sanguine race, and in reply to all cheerful views of the future, merely shrug their shoulders, and say, 'time will show'. How can it be otherwise with people who cheerfully put up with Cutting's line of broken-down omnibuses, and jog and jingle into town every day, without a groan, over dislocating roads and at eight miles an hour, exposed to draughts, dust, and a degree of stuffiness in those ancient arks that would create a revolution on the Bayswater Road! Here you may meet fat Malay matrons, jammed side by side with unctuous officials, and mal-odorous nurses reeking with cocoanut oil, who almost poison our merchant princes. Our local millionnaire, though he owns half the village, is made of too tough a fibre to start a gig of his own, but he wisely sits close to the door, and monopolizes the first whiff of such air as ever struggles in to ventilate the vehicle. On the roof young Africa stretches its long limbs, and smokes sadly and solemnly all the way into town; and though the inside passengers are polite enough in all conscience to such ladies as venture to travel with them, woe betide the unfortunate damsels who enter such headachy precincts, and expect to preserve their tempers as well as their dresses from being crushed and despoiled by the way.

Whenever my dear old friend, Mrs. S— (I have only known her a week) has occasion to do a little shopping, she always puts on an old bonnet on her head, and carries a smart new one in its box on her lap, so as to neutralize the dust; and then she pops into the first shop where she is known, and emerges like an elderly butterfly, quite spruce and gay, upon the town. Can you conceive anything more ridiculous than a solemn party of gentlemen *in shocking bad hats*, sitting half benumbed in one of these drafty vans for more than eight miles, trying to converse in short, spasmodic jerks, pitched in a high key, and then all of them rushing into Cairncross's tart-shop to find their best beavers wherein to transact their business, and again doff them on their return journey? And yet — assures me that this is a sight which can be seen any day by an observant traveller; it provokes comparison with the humblest of railways at home.

Our village at night is musical with the croaking of frogs, the maddening horns of the fish-cart drivers, and the barking of discontented dogs, baying 'their monstrous melodies to the moon'. A quiet game at whist, however, has brought us in contact with some few pleasant people who are musically inclined, and so we escape sometimes from the jarring discords of the animal world to the soothing strains of Mozart and Beethoven. The contrast is delicious, and I am quite sure the only way to really enjoy good music, is to taste it over a cup of good tea – flavoured with village scandal – and partake of it as we do with open windows, and our chairs ranged in the moonlight. Ah, my dear —, why cannot we do in England what they do in France, and very often have 'a feast of reason and a flow of soul' without putting ourselves to such frightful expense and trouble over our parties, our 'drums', and our balls! A few choice sandwiches, some good lemonade, cakes, fruit, coffee, tea, and harmless pleasantry, and surely our accomplished women ought to succeed as well in England in entertaining company as kind-hearted, simple souls succeed in this obscure corner of the world. It is not the will nor the power of pleasing, but the manner that is wanting. We lean too much to show and display. We vie too much with each other in extravagance and plate, until all enjoyment is banished from the heart of the hostess, and the guests make silent comparisons, instead of talking and laughing, as we meant them to do. As Froissart long ago said – 'Why do we amuse ourselves so sadly?' Why cannot we drop in of an evening quietly upon each other, and exchange experiences of thought, of reading, of sentiment, or of travel, without fussing so terribly about dress and previous notice? Where the French converse freely, we stare at photographs, and the result is we may be very well informed, but we are awful slow coaches. Cannot we change this? I mean to try.

28th January.— I must now give you an account of last week's round of dissipation. We have been 'assisting' at a birthday feast at Newlands, which was very well worth attending. At three p.m. a fat old butler in white cotton gloves, and with a face shining as if black-leaded, announced dinner to be served, – and the founder of the feast, with a grinning young Sambo at his back, waving off the flies with a bunch of ostrich feathers, took his place at the head of his hospitable table, and glanced with pardonable pride at the goodly array of viands and olive branches ranged round the board. We mustered eight-and-thirty souls! What boots it to tell of the curries and ragouts, the joints and *entrées*, the poultry, the pastry and game of the first course, – of the jellies and custards, puddings, tarts, and curious confectionery of the second, – or of the endless display of grapes and berries, figs, peaches, pine apples, and melons, at the dessert; of how one mixed his guavas with his sherry, how another used salt with his orange, and a third sprinkled pepper over his musk melon, sipping his claret at the same time. Suffice it to say, it was nearly six ere all the proper toasts were honoured, and the gentlemen joined us. Then there was a general cry for the musicians to strike up and *'spuil a bietjie'*. Speedily a clever stringed band came to the front, and fiddled away at whatever was called for, entirely by ear. Jigs, melodies, and polkas followed in rapid succession. Then a supply of beer was served out to them, during the consumption of which the younger folk sent off urgent dispatches to their dancing neighbours to come and join them, and then dashed with the utmost zeal into the circling waltz and fatiguing gallopade. Then the servants – male and female – pressed forward to see the fun, and being descried, were ordered by the old squire to stand forth and dance away for their master's amusement, while the old people placidly looked on and enjoyed their pipes and coffee *à la turque*. The new arrivals brought with them fresh musicians and vigorous limbs, and so master and valet, maiden and maid, footman and groom, and pages of high and low degree, in inextricable confusion, went footing it and capering it over the smoothly-mown lawn, until even the coarse grass broke out into a violent perspiration, and the falling dew drove the company within doors. Nor would they stop here! Their dancing blood being thoroughly up, a ball-room was soon improvised by moving all the heavy furniture out of the great hall, and submitting its highly-polished oak floor to the indignity of being trampled and jumped upon by stalwart cavaliers and heavy boots, and having its lustre smirched by the ponderous Balmorals of more than one buxom wench!

In dancing at the Cape, there is no mincing the matter, no solemn pretence of being pleased, no spasm of the lip and inward groaning of the spirit, but real, downright, honest, unrestrained play of limb and of countenance, producing a wholesome perspiration and developing a hearty appetite for supper. And as with the masters, so with the servants in the capacious kitchen, where the sable attendants plunged and curvetted, pranced and leaped, shrieked, laughed, slapped their hands and soles and knees, and indulged in such eccentric gymnastic feats amongst their demented selves, that it seemed as if Bedlam had broken loose and no keepers were to be found for love or money.

About ten o'clock somebody started the idea of hunting up porcupines, and in a few minutes the courtyard presented an assemblage of the most villainous, ill-bred mongrels possible to conceive. Yelping and howling, and gnashing their teeth, and making night hideous with their cries, they were soon slipped on to the spoor, and started off in pursuit. A number of gentlemen followed the chase in the moonlight, and finally brought the vermin to bay close to an old outhouse, where, — says, he made a truly gallant defence worthy of a better beast. The row that now ensued as he stood, fronting the dogs, with all his bristles or quills on the *qui vive*, protesting against such abominable treatment, was something excruciating; and such a hullabaloo was made, that no one was sorry when one of the youngsters put a stop to it, by giving the porcupine a slight tap on the nose with his stick, thereby laying him dead at his feet.

CHAPTER SEVEN

Hospitality at Constantia and a picnic at Kalk Bay

10th February, 1862

What a splendid thing is rest! Next to sleep, there nothing more delightful than giving yourself up entirely to laziness for a season, and dozing the hours away in dreamy do-nothingness under trees that shield you not only from the glare, but also render more fragrant the glorious fresh free air that here fans you into Paradise. I fancy I must have some gipsy blood in my veins somewhere, for after every fresh burst of energy, all I care for is to be thoroughly idle, and rest on my elbows looking out of a wigwam! To watch a black fellow smoking at the door is his '*pondockie*', is to envy him the supreme nonchalance with which he treats time, duty, and place. Happiness seems to float around him – there is a blissful turning up of the eye-balls, and a suggestive twist of the lips, which speak volumes for his thorough enjoyment of his old clay pipe; and then he is not selfish – but allows his better half to enjoy her short pipe too! Our present quarters are within a convenient distance of a number of huts and mealie patches belonging to native farm labourers, and I have ample opportunities of studying the domestic economy of our coloured neighbours. Their fat little jack-puddings of children run about in the scantiest of shirts, and pick up their dinners apparently just as the fowls do, by clucking over everything eatable they may come across. The moment they see us coming, they scamper away like a lot of kids into these huts and peep out at us from their dark and well-smoked interiors, like Robinson Crusoe's goat in the cave – all eyes and gleaming white teeth. If you, however, hold up sixpence and say you want to buy some watermelons, out they will all come again, one after another, until the whole family are dispersed over the roughly enclosed garden, looking up the ripest fruit to sell. Each little vagabond shouts with glee that his melon is riper that the others, and there you will see them knocking away at the thick green rinds with their knuckles as if they were doctors sounding your chest, until the mother authoritatively steps in, gives the various specimens of melons a good shake to detect a hollow sound, and then runs the blade of a knife a couple of inches into the interior of the likeliest one as it rests upon the ground, so as to pull out a small plug of red pulp as a test of its forward condition. The melon is then twisted off the stalk, well banged about over the head of the noisiest brat to prove its ripeness, and tucked under the arms of the biggest, like a helpless baby in very short clothes, for safe conveyance to our kitchen.

You can't conceive how difficult it is for a gentleman to carry a watermelon for you. It is too big for his pocket – too heavy for one hand, and excessively inconvenient for two. It is hard, smooth, and slippery, – in fact, a huge dead pig of a fruit, with nothing to grasp firmly but a ridiculous little tail of a stalk. If you carry it in both arms, you are sure to laugh at your own solemn sense of the trust imposed on you, and let it fall in consequence; but the black fellows just clap it on their woolly heads or shoulders, and walk off smiling, like milkmaids with their pails. Need I say this fruit is delicious. On the hottest day, when the thick rind feels warm to the touch, the pink pulp within is almost as cool as raspberry ice – melting in your mouth, very sweet and delicious, and full of a thin juice, – hence the name. It grows like a cucumber in long trailing plants, with large leaves and a trumpet-shaped flower. I have seen them spread out over the sandy soil for more than twenty feet, and the funniest thing about them is that they grow just as well without being watered as when regularly soaked every day.

Of course, the gardens are not very neatly kept – nothing at the Cape ever is; but a favourite device is to plant mealies, – that is, Indian corn, in short rows, about a yard apart, and under their shelter from wind and sun, cultivate beans, peas, onions, leeks, &c. The soil must be good, though it looks poor and white, as the gardens everywhere are full of vegetables, and quite account for the sleekness and sloth of their lucky proprietors. These mealies can be eaten in two or three ways. When young and full of milk, they are stripped of a sort of silky brown beard in which they are wrapped by nature, and either boiled or highly scorched before a slow fire till they turn brown, and so eaten hot for breakfast. When fully ripened, the cobs are allowed to dry in heaps, and then the grains are easily brushed off the core by a sweep of the thumb, and so made ready for market as food for poultry and cattle, as well as for the natives. Our youngsters like them best raw, and are never happier than when gnawing a soft mealie cob: so that what with pumpkins, mealies, and melons, they are growing as round as young Kafirs, and not a whit less healthy.

Friday, 21st February.— The mail still brings us news of this miserable American war. Will they never stop fighting? It is horrible to think of the utter misery which will be the ultimate fate of the poor Southern gentry, after all their trials and privations, in defence of their right to secede. In this Colony people take the deepest interest in European politics, and you would be surprised at the eagerness with which everything is here discussed the moment the arrival of the steamer has caused a lot of extras and supplements to be distributed over town and country. All our sympathies here are with the South, and no wonder. *** The death of Prince Albert also has made a great sensation.

To turn to home news, accept my best thanks for the admirable manner in which you executed my troublesome little commissions. Everything arrived in capital condition by the *Dane*, and does credit to your packing.

And so you all approved of the Constantia, Van Rhum, and other cordials sent you on trial? Well, you are not singular in your taste, for I am quite of your opinion that they are very nice. The farms which are specially noted for these liqueurs are favourite points of interest to visitors at the Cape, and in many respects are well worth the journey to such out-of-the-way spots. To take you there quickly from Wynberg, we have only to order our horses, and scamper off in the direction of Hout Bay to reach it in half an hour. The route is not particularly interesting, stretching as it does across three or four miles of sandy plain, well clothed with heather and protea bushes; but after a sharp canter you take a turn to the left and enter a long avenue, which leads up straight to the hospitable château of Great Constantia. The courtyard here is graced by a number of very fine old oaks in double file, and is bounded on one side by outbuildings, and on the other by a low, whitewashed wall, which encloses large vineyards, full of short, stumpy little bushes, well furnished with big bunches of yellow and purple grapes. All the vines are planted in long, straight, regular rows, about a yard apart, and are entirely free of props or supports of any kind. You are made welcome to the establishment as a matter of course, the horses are off-saddled and led to the stables, and you are invited inside, there to admire the spacious apartments and enjoy their coolness after your hot ride; or, if not unwilling to tuck up your habit under your arm, and take a survey of the estate, you are treated to a scramble through the vineyards, at the risk of spoiling your palate for many a day, by injudicious tasting of every kind of grape submitted to you, to say nothing of the luscious peaches that almost melt in your mouth.

Not to bore you with the details of wine-making, suffice it to say that the Constantia grapes are not picked until they have almost shrivelled into raisins, and that they don't make very much wine every year; but you would be amazed at the extraordinary size of the huge casks and elephantine tuns ranged in order in the enormous cellars, which are very long, very dark, and almost chilly in comparison with the blaze of sunshine outside.

Nothing can exceed the hearty good nature with which you are shown round the property by the younger members of the family, who talk a polyglot patois with their numerous daily visitors; and when you think of starting home again, after sipping samples from various brands, and duly admiring their taste, they very considerately invite you into the house again, where you make the acquaintance of ladies who are as pleasant as they are unassuming, and who must be heartily tired of their daily routine of duties in the hard work of entertainment. As the rooms gradually fill with company, you are asked to adjourn to a large saloon, where you find a capital luncheon laid out – an every-day business arrangement, combining hospitality and trade principles, and rendered necessary by the long distance from any hotel. The carriage-loads of strangers who turn up on fine days at all hours of the morning in drags, tandems, carts, and four-in-hand could not well otherwise be accommodated except in this generous fashion; and the people who come in them are certainly extraordinary customers in every sense of the word. May their numbers never grow less.

There was no wine-pressing going on when we were there, but later in the season, the big tubs will be filled by a mob of perspiring labourers, who will parody Macaulay's lays as to the must foaming round the feet of laughing boys. Mr. Cloete smiled at the idea of there being either poetry or fun in the treading of the wine-press, but assured us as it was very hard work indeed, and I should think anything but nice to lookers-on.

On our way back we looked in upon his neighbour, Mr. Van Reenen, for the especial purpose of seeing a curious oak tree, which spreads out at about twelve feet from the ground into a huge fork, and here they have set up a table and benches and turned it into a summer house, to reach which you have to ascend a ladder and enjoy in imagination the feelings of the second Charles under similar circumstances. In every other respect the farm details were the same, but on a smaller scale; but both proprietors vie each other in their civility to strangers, and are admirable specimens of the good old colonist, of Van der Stell pattern.

As to the 'Van Rhum', some say it is made out of 'naartjee' peel – a species of mandarin orange, – while others tell me it is prepared from certain herbs, only known to the initiated. Anyhow, when well prepared, it is capital, and I am glad to hear Aunt M. so thoroughly appreciated its flavour. *** It is a favourite cordial after dessert, and our old friend Mrs. M— makes it to perfection.

Thursday, 27th February.— We have been having a capital picnic yesterday down by the seaside at Kalk Bay. The day was gloriously fine, and, as is the custom here, we were told to be ready by eight, and bring anything we pleased in the way of dishes and baked meats. Our hostess charged herself with the care of the drinkables, and engaged to call for us in one of Cutting's old omnibuses, with its special team of six lively screws, and a nondescript driver. Accordingly, at the appointed hour, ourselves and hamper were carefully packed into the roomy old ark, and, in the company of at least a dozen young people, we were pleasantly jolted down to the appointed rendezvous. As we had only eight or nine miles to go, we amused ourselves in the usual fashion common to such occasions, and were not sorry when at length the sight of the dark blue sea suddenly burst upon us, with a delightful salt breeze to cool our foreheads as we passed through the toll-gate at Muisenberg.

Kalk Bay is a little fishing hamlet, consisting of a few old-fashioned Dutch houses, and a dozen or so of fishermen's huts straggling for a mile between the rocky beach, and the bleak precipitous mountains that rise up almost immediately behind it. It is accounted a very healthy place, and is the favourite resort to well-to-do people, who like to exchange the ennui and smells of a hot town for the more bracing breezes and even stronger scents of the sea-side. The scenery, but for the wide expanse of blue water, is very dreary and ugly. Not a tree to be seen – the bushes stunted and starved, and behind the houses rise up bare brown knolls or 'koppies', highly suggestive of mineral wealth, but otherwise very bleak and desolate. Were it not for the sea breeze, it would be impossible to live here a week; yet for an occasional visit it is full of amusement – the smallest incident going a very long way. Our arrival soon made us the observed of all observers, and I should have taken refuge in the wayside hotel but for two reasons – first, that nobody could be found to join me; and secondly, that the hotel, as usual, would have had little or nothing to give us for breakfast until the boats had come in, and as this would have taken time, we decided upon making a descent upon the coast, and cooking our own meals in *al fresco* fashion on the rocks. Here, then, in a shorter time than it takes me to write it, we found ourselves like a set of gipsies encamped. The horses were at once knee-haltered and turned loose, the servants sent searching for wood and bushes, the old caravan emptied of its contents; and what with coffee, eggs, porter, cold tongue, ham, and chicken, a very admirable *déjeuner a la fourchette* was rapidly improvised. There is nothing to give you an appetite like sea air and an early ride, and you would have laughed heartily at the *bizarre* nature of the articles severally furnished by the members of the picnic towards the feast.

After breakfast we all dispersed in different directions in search of the picturesque, – I, for my own part, going in quest of shells, which I had promised to the children, and which are to be found in great number and variety in queer out-of-the-way nooks and corners. To reach these you have to scramble over rocks that are jumbled about even more wildly than on the top of Table Mountain, only that all the gaps between are full of sea-water, clearer, perhaps, than looking-glass.

Any sand or soil that may once have covered these rocks has since disappeared, and now the waves come and dash their spray high up in the air, almost over the roadway.

The noise of the breakers is very great, and yet, after a time so little regarded that, happening to sit down in a cosy little nook, watching the sea gulls and fishing-boats, I must have dropped off to sleep, lulled thereto by the sunshine and the ceaseless roar and dash of the surf, – for I was suddenly aroused by a shower of spray in my face, and a peal of laughter above me. I jumped up, rubbing my eyes, and then discovered the tide to be rising, and that a stronger wave than usual had almost deluged me, to the huge delight of friends, including my husband – who were enjoying my discomfiture not very far off. Dripping as I was, I remembered the old saying that 'Salt water never gives cold', and, like the little boy in Punch, determined to run about and dry myself; so to that end, gathered up my skirts, and strolled on to a little plot of delicious white beach close to the church; and there the shells strewed the sands so thickly, that you could not resist going down on your hands and knees and filling your pockets with flotsam and jetsam of almost microscopic minuteness. I thought of my little ones at home, and so grasped all I could get, especially pouncing upon the prickly sea eggs, and a very delicate dark-blue shell, most lively and bright, and held by many to be identical with the ancient Tyrian dye. Some of the shells were like coins, and some like screws, but all were gleaming with the lights of opal and mother-of-pearl, and made a very pretty collection indeed.

A little further on brought us to the Fishery, where we found a 'most ancient and fish-like smell', highly significant of rough ways and means of cure. The boats were just coming in as we got opposite to this inlet of the sea. They were laden to the brim with many curious specimens of fish, which were immediately tumbled into dirty old carts, and driven off rapidly to Cape Town for sale. Of course we bought a bundle or two of

silver fish, and it was not very long before they were broiling on the embers of our mid-day lunch. Our flow of spirits at this meal was almost as wonderful as our morning appetites, and it must have been many a long day since the echoes of the old cave were so rudely awakened as by our bursts of laughter and of song.

When the day began to get a little cooler, we scrambled down to the rocks again to search for the very lovely and delicate sea-weeds blooming in every little pool, and one of the gentlemen of our party lighted upon a most horrible creature called a 'catfish', but which ought more properly to have been named a 'sea devil', if there be such a thing – as it was all arms and legs, and huge goggle-eyed head. This frightful-looking creature quite cured us of any further desire to dip our hands into the briny pools, as we were told that if it caught anything living in its grasp It never let go till all its limbs were severed from its body. What a pleasant bathing companion to be introduced to!

Down at Kalk Bay the chief amusement is not to bathe but to stand out upon the rocks, with an immense bamboo rod and line, and catch fish in the broken water. The only place where there is a nice sandy beach is over at Muisenberg, extending from near the toll-gate as far as the strand of Somerset West, and there ought to be a large number of bathing machines drawn up in line, but nothing of the kind is known here. This beach seems to be a favourite place for hauling big nets, and I am told the contents of the seines are enough sometimes to puzzle a naturalist, including toadfish, dogfish, catfish, and juvenile sharks. Extending as it does in a gentle curve for miles, and perfectly firm when moistened by the retiring tide, the Muisenberg beach must be a capital place for a gallop, as you can't hurt yourself if you should fall, and a run-away horse cannot go very far without stopping of his own accord to take breath. *** Many ladies bring their horses down with them, and two or three riding parties passed us while we were busy getting ready to return. And so as the sun was slowly sloping to the West, we gathered up our traps, our baskets, and our spoils, and, with aching backs and sunburnt faces, gladly took our seats in the wretched old omnibus – only too happy to reach home, take a warm bath, and so to bed and the land of dreams.

Friday, 14th March, 1862.— There is some talk of our going to the Frontier, and as yet I have not half exhausted the various places of interest in the Western Province. We have still to see Stellenbosch, and the wine districts of Paarl and Worcester, and look forward to an early trip to these old-fashioned parts – so capitally described by Lady Anne Barnard. Till then let me introduce you to other more immediate surroundings. Just behind our house are collected huge waves of the purest white sand, which are slowly being drifted from the shores of False Bay by the action of south-east winds across to Table Bay, and threaten to engulf every house that comes within their influence. These sand-dunes are at least twelve to thirteen feet high, and are most extraordinary freaks of nature. For years it puzzled everybody how to fix them, until the late Colonial Secretary hit upon the device of planting them with Hottentot fig – a wild succulent plant, like a lot of fingers moulded in green jelly, and which will grow anywhere; and now many of these hills have retained their old shapes, and are quite covered with his hardy creeper. It is across these hills that the members of the Cape Fox Hunting Club in olden times were wont to chase the nimble jackal of the country, and many a good story have we heard of the extraordinary performances of old Indians in these very unlikely waves of sand. These 'dunes' practically extend for miles to Zekoe Vlei, or Hippopotamus Lake, and across these Flats, in times of old, lions used to range concealed in the thick masses of reed, which stick up stiffly everywhere like the hair of a man who has seen a ghost! These 'Flats', too, are dotted with springs or 'vleis' (good-sized basins, bearing upon their oily, still surfaces many pretty water plants), and are graced with lovely heaths, dewplants, and an infinitude of bulbs in blue, purple, white, and rose colours. Through them flows a stream called the Black River, which stains everything deep red, and which sluggishly finds its way into the lagoons of Salt River. To scamper across these Flats is like riding on the top of a Scotch or Yorkshire Moor, and only for the scream of some excited *kalkoontjie* circling over its nest in the heather, the scene is as quiet and subdued as the heart of man can desire. The view is bounded by lofty hills, at the foot of which are to be found Stellenbosch and Somerset West, and close to the latter Hanglip Point, the scene of the loss of the *Birkenhead**, with troops.

In three hours you can reach Eerste River by cart from our place, though the new railway soon promises to do it in one, but it takes you a good hour's drive further before you reach Somerset West. This is a very pretty and wealthy little village on the high road to the wool districts, and owes much to its charming position, and the admirable management of its interests by its founder – old Simon Van Der Stell. The country all about is cut up into large farms, but the chief of these – both for wood and water – is the splendid farm of old Mr. Theunissen, formerly the summer palace of the famous Dutch Governor, Van der Stell, and built upon a scale of magnificence that has rarely been equalled elsewhere at the Cape. Mr. T— was kind enough to show us a book printed in 1712, wherein is marked a full plan of the house as it existed in Van der Stell's time. The mansion, which stands in the middle, was then surrounded by a belt of defences of which nothing now remains but the central building. The saloons are of very great height, delightfully cool and well ventilated, and the ceilings made of camphor-wood, just as at Constantia the rafters were made out of trunks of silver trees. In the courtyard stand some gigantic camphor-wood trees, brought directly from Japan some seventy years ago, and now increased to a girth of twenty-four feet, but I am afraid to

---

* This is one of the few errors as to matters of detail into which the Lady occasionally falls. The *Birkenhead* was wrecked at Danger Point, some thirty or forty miles further along the coast. –Ed. "C.M.M"

say how high they are. They are the only ones in the Colony, and are well worth a visit. But what makes this place so pretty is the abundance of fresh water flowing in a deep but narrow stream round it as a boundary. The park-like meadows and gardens are admirably kept and well irrigated, and the sea itself is plainly visible about three miles off, so that it is a residence fit for a prince, with plenty of fishing, shooting, and sea air to please all tastes.

A little further on and the road takes you up Sir Lowry Pass, which is a magnificent mountain road, with frightful precipices on the one side, leading to the Caledon district. The view from the top of this Pass is very lovely, and is grander and more extensive, if possible, than from the Kloof Road. It embraces a range almost as great as from the top of Table Mountain, and, like that, is very weird and weather beaten on the summit, dwarfing even the Lion's Head.

As there is a capital little inn at Somerset West, we stopped here a few days last week, and greatly enjoyed our bathing on the 'Strand'. Here we found a number of Cape farmers, with their wagons and tents set up on the sands, camping out as cooly as if they belonged to the sea, and accompanied by their families from Stellenbosch and the surrounding districts. The matrons and boer servant girls wore the funniest head dresses and sun-shades conceivable, while the men sprawled about under the lee of their wagons, just as boatmen would creep under their boats at Broadstairs and Deal. As the sands are very fine and the beach shelving, it is a thousand pities nobody has been enterprising enough to start a dozen of bathing machines, so as to improve its great natural capacities as a watering place. *** I am sure they would take everybody's fancy here when once started.

CHAPTER EIGHT

Stellenbosch, Wellington and the Paarl

9th April, 1862

And so you wish to hear more about the people, and what sort of creatures our big-wigs are! Well, the fact is, everybody here is on such familiar terms with his neighbours, and the families are so intricately intermarried and related to one another, that it requires a cleverer head than mine to detect the existence of the upper ten thousand from the gentry and middle classes. We are all loyally attached to the Crown of course, but we are all easy-going republicans at heart; and, except at the opening and closing of Parliament, I believe nobody dreams of quarrelling about seats in the synagogue, and precedence before the Viceroy. If there be any heart-burning at balls because the Chief Secretary waltzes too frequently with some frisky matron, or the Treasurer-General, or Auditor-General, or Collector of Customs, or even the learned Attorney-General takes some pretty young creature in to supper, to the neglect of more fully blown wall-flowers, the matter is so ridiculous that I should think nobody gives it a thought. For although these titles sound high and grand enough, the high officials themselves are such meek and mild, not to say rusty bodies in appearance, that to be jealous of their notice would indeed be the height of absurdity.

There is one member of the Government who is really *distingué*, and that is Mr. P—, a handsome old Irishman of the old school. Nothing can be more delightful than to have a talk with him; and an after-dinner speech from Mr. P— is truly a feast of wit and delicate humour. He is one of the social 'institutions' of the Cape, and what the Americans would call a very 'remarkable man', – in short, a personage of whom everybody is justly proud; but his health is so broken by hard work, that he is going to leave us shortly, though everyone hopes for his speedy return. *** As for the crowd of merchants and merchants' sons – and, for the matter of that, merchants' daughters – there is nothing about them to distinguish them from the usual attendants upon balls and dinners at home. They dress in quiet but very good taste, are much taken up with English and foreign politics, and sedulously avoid any allusion to business; not that their business is anything to be ashamed of, but simply, I suppose, because they don't want to bore us about punjums and baftas, and the fall in wool and feathers. *** In the eyes of some, it is just possible that the women are vapid and easily pleased, – they are certainly pale and far from plump; but if neat figures, good dancing, and unusually bright eyes have no attraction for men, their naval and military partners deserve to be jumped round the room by romping 'Blowsabellas', and dragged off their feet by ruddy Dutch milkmaids.

I notice that very little jewellery is worn here. A simple wreath or spray of artificial flowers in the glossy dark hair, or a red and white camellia at the back of the head, are of themselves sufficient to set off the very bright eyes of colonial girls. Brown and grey eyes predominate. Blue eyes and fair hair are generally imported; but blue eyes and black hair, as in Ireland, are seldom seen combined. The clans of Scotland are not more numerous than the members of the C—, M—, Van R—, Van dB—, and B— families, who jostle against you wherever you turn; and it is amusing to watch the bewildered looks of strangers who try to find their partners when there are perhaps a dozen young ladies of the same name in the room. I see that Lady Ann Barnard was disappointed in not finding Cape women handsomer; she considered them to be deficient in real beauty having – as she says – 'no countenance, no manner, no grace, no charms – though plenty of good looks and the freshness of health, with a vulgar smartness accompanying it, which show the torch of Prometheus which animated them to be made of mutton tail. What they want most is shoulders and softness of manners. The term "Dutch doll' was quite explained to me when I saw their make, and recollected the dolls; but what is most exceptionable about them is their teeth and the size of their feet.'

This was written in 1797, when of course there was but little intercourse with Europe, and might have with equal justice have been said of American ladies then. Certainly, the fashions are not neglected here now. The ladies wear very pretty bonnets and boots and gloves; and as for Dutch dolls with pink cheeks, flaxen hair, shapeless noses, and general air of imbecility, I, for one, have not seen any in society or out of it. If I did not know the author of Auld Robin Gray to be a consummate quiz by her letters, I should say she must have been slightly prejudiced at first against the Cape people by the coolness of her reception. Be this as it may – 'nous avons changé tout cela', – and I again assert that Cape girls compare favourably with English countrywomen, and generally marry very young.

As for the working classes – except among the negroes – you seldom see a thoroughly ugly face. The quadroons, if not fair, are at least as handsome as gipsies, and among the paler Malays I have even seen thoroughly good-looking features. The negroes, of course, and the cross-breeds, are ridiculously plain, with enormous mouths, woolly hair, but oh, such magnificent teeth! – white, even, and gleaming. They are all, however, fond of ease and laziness. Upon the frontier districts, where the savages dispense with tailors, and are said to wrap themselves with as much dignity in a greasy red blanket as any noble Roman in his toga, I have no doubt I shall come across some very fine specimens of undiluted barbarism; but down in the Western Provinces – formerly the stronghold of the slave proprietors – slavery has set its mark upon the coloured races, and made them look as happy as if they had no cares. Blessed with fine teeth, bright skins of bronze, capital figures, and undeniably good-humoured eyes, they represent a striking contrast to the toil-worn, stooping, shambling English operative, with his ill-made fustian garments. With farm-servants, the favourite dress seems to be made up of a full suit of currypowder moleskin, or brown sheepskin and corduroy, admirably set off by a bunch of grey or black ostrich feathers in their wide-awake hats, a brilliant cotton kerchief for the head, or a gorgeous waistcoat with glass buttons. In the country round about Somerset and Stellenbosch, where we have been gadding about this fortnight, you see nothing worn on the feet but 'veldschoens' – that is, leather sandals, extremely soft, and well adapted for walking on sand and grass. Most of the farmers wear them, and are the probable cause of the enormous feet distinctive of these stalwart worthies.

Monday, 14th April.— For the last few days the weather has been showery and delightfully cool; and the rain has washed off all the summer dust from the hedges and trees of our country cousins. We have extended our tour to the Paarl and Wellington, and hope to get as far as Worcester and Caledon, before leaving for the frontier.

Our first excursion was, of course, to some friends at Stellenbosch – a really very pretty place, about thirty miles from Cape Town. The village, embowered in trees, is quaintly Dutch, full of gables and stables, and is as neat as whitewash and green paint can make its rows of picturesque brown-thatched old houses.

All the streets are shaded with double rows of oaks, and kept cool and clean by water-furrows, full of clear sparkling water from the river. The place supports a large population, who, however, do not appear much in public, and it has a sleepy, well-to-do air in the neatness of its gardens, and the general look of prosperity about the cattle and horse-teams; but it lies too low ever to be quite healthy. There are some fine farms in the neighbourhood – with many excellent descendants from first-class *refugée* French families for their frank and good-tempered owners. *** I am puzzled to say what many of them do for their livelihood, but I presume they grow market produce, and, from the number of vineyards, and orchards, and kitchen-gardens studding the vale, there must be a fair field for making wine and brandy, and preserving dried fruits, &c. Trade there is none.

From Stellenbosch it is a fair morning's drive to the Paarl – through a billowy and scrubby country, where the road, in its devious course, gives you capital bird's-eye views of orange farms, and many very charmingly situated country places. The best country here is folded behind and between undulating hills, and consists of a series of treeless downs until you reach the steep vineyards of the Paarl, where you find yourself skirting the base of a very rocky granite hill, scarred all over with winding foot-paths,

zigzagging up to two enormous grey boulders or bosses perched on its top; and which, from their supposed resemblance to gigantic pearls, give the village its name. At a distance they look like two enormous quinces. It must be an awfully hot place in summer, for even the vineyards look scorched up, and the vineleaves are red as beetroot.

From the stoep of its chief hotel or boarding-house, it is great fun to watch the young farmers of the Paarl ambling past upon their pet horses. Every youngster has his nag, and knows how to manage him, but they have very clumsy seats, and are very poor hands at showing off before strangers. How shall I describe the nonchalant air with which they rein their horses in with sharp bits, until their lips touch their breasts, and their necks are made to arch like a sickle – while at the same time they are vigorously fretted with the spur, so as to cause them to prance and kick up a dust? Nobody seems to walk. Even the black fellows prefer stretching themselves out at full length on the floor of a slow bullock dray, to walking from one end of the village to the other; and when we sauntered down that tremendous long street we were well stared at by dozens of intensely respectable old fogies, every one of whom appeared to be in mourning, and wore at least six inches of crape round his broad-brimmed white beaver. The main street is nearly six miles long, and bordered all

down its dusty length by fine capacious houses, standing in their own green compounds, and well sheltered by avenues of oak and fir; and the long vista is terminated by an extraordinary bridge, like a wooden caterpillar crawling over an acre of stale loaves of bread. Who could have dreamed of such a nightmare of a bridge, or of such an unusual crop of round stones in the bed of a respectable river? The tawny water just now is conspicuous for its absence, though, as usual, the washerwomen are banging about the linen terribly on the stones, as if to punish them for being so dry; but in winter time the river comes down with frightful velocity and volume, tearing up the trees, and always more or less changing the course of the stream. Meanwhile, the rickety old bridge stands on long stilts, and is a terror to timid souls who fear to cross it when most required. It is indeed fearfully and wonderfully made, and worthy of a council of demented civil engineers!

While at the Paarl, we gathered much amusement from the pastoral scenes near the market-place after sunset and sunrise. Many wagons, with their loads, would then be outspanned, and drawn up in an irregular square, each with its long trough, or manger, made out of canvas, fixed on either side of the pole, out of which, perhaps, a dozen horses or mules would be feeding in a desperate hurry to get through their scant allowance of chaff and oats. Between and near the wheels could be seen groups of chattering natives, in their battered felt and straw hats, squatting round their crackling fires of bush and thorntree, cooking coffee and enjoying a frugal supper. The fitful leaping and falling of the flames played fantastic tricks with their dusky features, and brought out into high relief their picturesque surroundings. What with the squealing of cattle, the barking of dogs, the loud laughter of the drivers and leaders comparing experiences, and the absence of drunkenness, the sight contrasted favourably with the market scenes of older countries; but the publicans and sinners are kept in capital order be a very energetic Dutch pastor, who has abolished canteens, and means to put down the coming Railway! This worthy is quite a character.

By cock-crow everybody is up and about. The produce is then sold by public auction, and seemed to me to realize ridiculously low prices. Then in a few hours the place would be quite cleared out, and while our Cape Town friends are still sleeping, the long trains of empty wagons, with their fine teams of oxen, – perhaps, twenty in number, would be slowly on their way home again. If there was a hitch on the road, crack, crack went the whips like pistolshots, mingled with furious abuse of lagging leaders or lazy wheelers, and a vigorous pounding forthwith with 'sjamboks', as the young masters or active drivers ran nimbly by the sides of the offenders, and thrashed them up the steep hills or through the heavy bits of sandy road with remorseless hands and unflagging tongues. Then, too, the morning air would be rent with the shrill cries of 'Bos*man*! Co*burg*! English*man*! Wit*foot*! trek, trek', in *alto crescendo*, each word being accompanied by a flourish of the enormous bamboo-handled whips of the Colony, long enough to reach the flanks of ten oxen at one skilful blow, and severe enough to lay the skin open, if the owner were so minded. Poor oxen, they look so calm and patient, with their mild eyes and dewy nostrils, soberly bending their necks to the yoke as they slowly and steadily pace on in apparent contempt of the lively teams of horses and skittish mules that pass them at a brisk trot! Yet they, too, get over a great deal of ground in the twenty-four hours; and although three miles an hour is not very fast travelling, it is surprising how long the same span of oxen can be kept at it, if the roads are not too hard, and there is enough of water and grass at the end of each day's journey.

For any one who wishes to see the country thoroughly and leisurely, there is nothing to beat the bullock-wagon, as it is steadily progressive, and serves for kitchen, house, and bed, making you thoroughly independent of hotels, and defying the roughest or sandiest roads with its broad wheels. It is far more comfortable than you can imagine it to be, but it is chiefly used by traders.

Thursday, 17th April. — In all our excursions to farms or up the hills, we used a cart and two horses; and it was wonderful what a lot of rough and quick work could be got out of a wiry couple of job animals who are accustomed to travel together. Once or twice we have been under obligations to farmers for the generous loan of a fine pair of prancing high-stepping grays or bays – full of corn, and evidently wanting work; but although they started generally in the wildest spirits, as if out for a spree, tearing at their bits, and snapping at each other in play, yet somehow they usually returned crestfallen, and scraping up the dust with their heels in the last stages of plethoric exhaustion. Not so with our ragged-looking, bright-eyed little hired Cossacks that we brought from Wynberg, too thin for beauty and too battered for show, but with just that spice of the Arab in their blood as will bring them back as fresh as when they started on a trip of forty miles or so – out and in. You would smile to see how game they are – how easily pleased! They need no careful rubbing down, for no sooner do we stop to outspan than off goes their harness, the halter straps are knotted round the knee, and they are cast adrift to forage for themselves, and hunt up a nice soft spot for a roll in the sand, where they can tumble about on their backs, and knock their heels together to their hearts' content for at least five minutes. A good shake all over then sets them on their legs again, and they are ready for another stage.

As it is actually raining today, everybody is in good spirits, except the raisinmakers; but the prospect of summer breaking up is too delicious to the baked-up inhabitants of this district not to be rejoiced over. It is wet enough to confine me to the house of our hostess, Mietje Langveldt, so I have been amusing myself by pumping the old lady most unmercifully as to the resources and curiosities of the neighbourhood, and I don't think she will be sorry when we set off on Saturday for Worcester to witness the gathering of the farmers to Easter Nachtmaal.

Wellington is about eight miles from the Paarl, and is merely a repetition of that village, but is better laid out. The two places are separated by a very fertile and prosperous valley – famous for its wine, fruit, horses, and the manufacture of strong wagons. All the farms we have visited were admirably managed; and we have been everywhere very well received, so I shall always speak well of its people. The village itself is a very hot place, and is well laid out and planted with trees, just as at Stellenbosch and the Paarl.

The finest outlet from this fertile valley is by a wonderful steep road, that has been carried by many a twist and loop across projecting spurs and the most fantastic mountain sides, until it finally attains to the top of Bain's Kloof, whence it is carried through a series of steep and narrow defiles for about eighteen miles to Darling Bridge over the Breede River, and so on to the plains of Worcester. From Wellington this road can be traced as a thin red line, cutting its way far up the purple and opal heights, until lost in the grey crags and ruins of an old convict-barrack on the top of the Pass.

We obtained a splendid view on Tuesday of all the corn and wine-growing districts lying behind the Paarl and around 'Riebeek's Kasteel', by ascending an extraordinary shaped mountain called the 'Groenberg', which is always green, and free from rocks, and covered with a thick felt of round bushes. From this point of view we could see Table Mountain and the Lion's Head and the broad deep-blue ocean beyond; and such an amazing number of farms and vineyards, like yellow and green lozenges in a patchwork quilt of brown and lavender-coloured bushes, as would surprise the good people of England.

Close by to this, and under Bain's Kloof, is the homestead of honest old Mr. M—, which we were pressed to visit; and we had the pleasure – after duly admiring the fine oaks and the well-cultivated grounds of this hale old gentleman – of sitting down to a midday meal, where our host and all his numerous family of sons, grandsons, and endless nephews and nieces, were seated round the same long table, with the German overseers and white servants of the farm at the bottom, below the salt. Some of the men just dined in their shirt sleeves, the day being hot, but everybody was preternaturally quiet, and nothing could be more sedate than the conduct of the youngsters, who solemnly bolted huge junks of stewed and boiled meat, heedless of seasoning and vegetables. The meal was certainly plentiful, but plain; the wine thin and watery, and not over clear; but the dessert was, as usual, very good and unusually ripe. The gardens were full of huge pumpkins, like the small bundles of wash-clothes we see perched on the heads of the native washer-women; and the fritters made from them were excellent. As most of the farmers understand English, even if they don't speak it, we had no difficulty in getting on with them; but they are very pertinacious in finding out whether you are married, and who your father was, and whether you have many children, &c., &c., all of which questions were satisfactorily answered for us by the jolly young Dutchman who drove us over from Wellington. Indeed, I quite won the heart of the hostess by my devotion to her butter and 'boer-brood', and when we left, the dear old soul gave me some excellent buck biltong and 'meibos', and promised to send me some sugar-bush syrup as a cure for cough and relaxed throat for my little girls. They are a proud and reserved people, but thoroughly kind if you don't give yourself airs, and avoid flippancy.

The plans of these farm-houses are the same everywhere – a long hall, double frontage, wide stoep, lofty rooms, thatched roofs, gable ends, and the kitchen and offices distinct. The stables and byres and straw-yards are very primitive. The delicious climate does everything; the gardens are full of produce, and an occasional jaunt to Cape Town is the only break to the monotony of farm life. You would be greatly amused at the cleverness of the herds, who, at milking time, would call out the right name of every calf out of perhaps fifty in the kraal, as each was required in its turn to join its mother, before she could be induced to yield her milk. Of course, each calf at once recognized its own parent, and skipped about in convulsions of delight while the pails were being filled.

We hear such stirring accounts of Worcester, that we mean to take advantage of the full moon, and start early on Saturday morning, so as to escape the heat of the day in the plains beyond, and see the farmers arrive in their wagons for the Communion service on Easter Sunday, – one of the great events of their year. If the weather clears up, we are promised a series of lovely views through Bain's Kloof, and a great variety of ferns and wild flowers. May our usual luck attend us, no dust and no wind!

Worcester Hotel, Saturday night, 19th April, 1862.— At last, here we are in fairyland! But oh, what a glorious succession of mountain vistas and Claudian landscapes have we not encountered by the way since leaving Wellington for this lovely spot! Here mountains are jumbled upon mountains in such an extraordinary mingling of sugarloaf, cockscomb, hogback, saddleback, and dragonback, with huge buttressed walls, broken-tooth ridges and snake-like spurs running into deep and mysterious valleys, that it is difficult to realize on paper the extraordinary belt of reft gigantic cliffs and rock-crowned hills by which the enormous level plains of Worcester are rigidly enclosed. Far as the eye can reach the jagged mountains pierce the clouds, and, like the cusps of a rocky coronet, glimmer and shimmer at sunrise and sunset with the tints of ruby, opal, and pearl round the massive features of the fairest country I have yet seen at the Cape. These are the mysterious blue mountains that puzzle us at Wynberg, and now that we are under them they seem more lovely than ever.

What is meant by a 'kloof' is the gap between two mountain chains that threaten to touch. At best, they are very narrow and tortuous, now contracting till the crags almost exclude the light, now opening into glorious vistas of rock and river. At Bain's Kloof we found the perfection of mountain scenery; and it is to me perfectly wonderful that no artist of merit has ever thought of studying these hill-side effects instead of drudging at Wales and Switzerland. With such a transparent atmosphere as prevails here, especially after a shower, when the sky is 'deeply, beautifully blue', and there is no dust to bother you, it is as easy to paint objects five miles off as it would be at fifty yards. They only need to be seen to be appreciated!

Well, at three in the morning we left our warm beds at old Mietjie Langeveldt's, had a cup of strong coffee and a biscuit, and started off in the brilliant moonlight with a cart and four fresh horses on our eight hours' journey to Worcester. The road began to rise almost at once, while the ravishing scenery, as we ecstatically toiled up the Pass, was simply indescribable in the chastened light of the dawn. Everything before us was wrapped in gloom; but it is impossible to do justice to the romantic beauty and depth and extent of the enormous valleys which were successively brought into view, as the excellent road twisted like a serpent in and out of the convolutions of the hills – the whole being brilliantly lit up by the moon. As the daylight grew stronger the sky, from blue and grey, melted into green and saffron, and finally rosy red; and in the far distance we could make out grey spectral lines, which our driver assured us were the hills of Piquetberg, about seventy miles off. Talk of the Splugen and the Vià Mala as much as you please, but I, for one, cannot conceive anything more perfectly beautiful than the play of light on the Drakenstein Mountains, when the moon beams pale before the sun's, followed by the sudden transfiguration of dim objects into rosy vapours and subtle essences, and the awakening of active life in the steaming valleys below. To the sound of the wind whistling overhead are to be added the ghostly whispering of the rushes, and the splashing of tiny waterfalls dashing headlong down the vales; and then almost suddenly we found ourselves on the top of the Pass – wild and weird to the highest degree, and with its crumbling sandstone rocks bleached and worn into the most astonishing shapes. Here they have placed a toll, and a few yards further on you obtain an immense panoramic view of Paarl, Wellington, Malmesbury, Simon's Berg, and the Constantia Hills, and can clearly discern Table Mountain and the Lion's Head in the extreme distance, glowing like a torch.

As the road is built up like a wall, you may fancy how steep are the valleys or series of valleys across which a solid viaduct has been made. They are at least two thousand feet deep, and are folded into each other like *interlaced fingers*. If you try to throw a stone across, it takes some time before it reaches the bottom, and woe betide the unfortunate wagoner who cannot stop his span in time when two wagons meet on the narrow Pass, and one obstinately refuses to yield the wall to the other. Our driver always blew his horn when he caught sight of a white wagon-tent in the distance, so as to avoid collision, and he almost frightened us by his terrible tales of the furious hurricanes which he had been sometimes obliged to encounter on these wind-torn heights. Luckily, the weather was clear and settled, but the morning so cold that we got out and walked a few miles down the Pass. Imperceptibly the road begins to descend for about nine miles, and is scarped out of enormous rocks, which, in every variety of shape and tint, threaten to topple over and bury the passing traveller in the ruins. Fancy thousands of crusty brown quartern loaves piled up to a dizzy height, and upon these Brobdignag loaves place squatting toads, or troops of mischievous monkeys playing at hide and seek, and you will have some idea of the extraordinary way in which these weather-worn and spectral groups of sandstone change their outlines as you proceed down the superb mountain defiles.

If you look over the sides of the viaduct, built up in strong and solid masonry by convict labour, and protected by large curbstones saved from the blasting, you gaze far down into deep brown pools, in which are reflected, as in a mirror, the steep sides of the well-wooded precipices beetling over the river, forming *perfect pictures*. Through the *débris* of fallen stones – bleached as white as ostrich eggs, through brakes of black palmiet cane, and through drifts of the purest white sand, wriggles and foams the noisy torrent. The dampish recesses are full of ferns and flowers. Tiny streams dribble and weep from under the roots of wayside trees. The whole prospect is fresh with the odours of paradise; and I gathered one lovely bright *yellow* heath, which I fancy must be very rare; while natural arches occur in one or two places where the rocks were too hard to blast away altogether. In short, the scenery was superb, and the rocks on the opposite side of the kloof were split up into square masses that looked as if the Titans had been building up steps to scale the sky, and had pointed the open joints and seams with a tree-bearing cement, so split are their crevices with vigorous shrubs. The scenery, though thus wild and fantastic, is, however, a fit prelude to the magnificent perspective of the Worcester range of mountains, which breaks in on you after reaching the accommodation-house kept by Messrs. Furney and Swain at the Darling Bridge. For miles the eye gazes with rapture on the superb picture, and if my lungs gloried in the pure mountain air, my sense of vision was equally charmed with the surprising freshness and beauty of the series of views now opened to us.

Here, of course, we stopped for an hour, to rest our horses and have breakfast. Everything was very primitive, but the people were very civil and most obliging for old bachelors; and held out prospects of good shooting to James, who has promised to return here for that purpose. Although we looked everywhere for baboons, we saw none; and beyond a few linnets, and a bird with a long tail, and another brown bird with a head shaped like a hammer and about as big as a rook, we saw but little signs of sport. I caught sight of three or four very pretty green lizards sunning themselves on the rocks, but they were off as quick as lightning and defied pursuit. So, too, of the butterflies, yellow and black. Again inspanning, we now crossed the Breede River, so called because it is very broad in the winter season, and is apt to overflow an enormous tract of level country after a couple of days' steady rain, when perhaps it may be three or four miles broad, though shallow. The road carries you in a nearly straight line to Worcester, forking away to Tulbagh and Ceres on the left, and passes through a brownish scrubby plain – dotted here and there with bright yellow patches of cornland – acres of green vineyards, and well-wooded homesteads, dark with orange, pomegranate, walnut, and apple trees. The great raisin district of Goudini stretches away on the right, while the horse and cattle breeders own much of the large properties on the left; but everywhere you miss signs of active labour, and are obliged to be content with pumpkins and oxen in the fields, instead of bands of reapers and creaking wains. We saw a few solemn old crows with white neckties, and a dignified secretary bird strutting after snakes, but no partridges nor pheasants fell to James's gun, for the simple reason that they never made an appearance. Nothing could exceed the slovenly style of farming everywhere prevalent, – mere scratches and patchwork in the wilderness, without any enclosures or fences.

Just as we were getting rather tired of the long straight road we caught a glimpse of the tower of the Dutch Reformed Church, which is the first thing seen of Worcester. You then turn the flank of a big brown hill, and the town suddenly lies before you – cool, green, and most refreshing to the eye, with the promise of grateful shade from the long avenues of firs.

CHAPTER NINE

Worcester is the prettiest place

21st April, 1862

If first impressions are worth anything, I think I must say that Worcester is the prettiest place I have ever seen. It is handsomely and regularly laid out, with fine broad streets, grassy side-paths, some good public buildings, and capital gardens well supplied with water. At the top of the principal street is the Drostdy House – a brick palace, erected in the times of Lord Charles Somerset as his shooting-box, and now occupied by a very polite old gentleman, who, as Civil Commissioner, lives there, and pays great attention to the handsome grounds attached to it. They are well worth a visit, and possess some enormous fig-trees, the fruit of which is as large as a small orange, but coarse and fleshy, with leaves as big as soup plates.

In the centre of the town is a very large common – or market-place – just as at Wynberg, and here they sell produce at very early hours indeed, and at prices absurdly low, – fowls, for instance, at 7d., and ducks a shilling a piece, and everything else in proportion; so that a small income here would go further in housekeeping than thrice the same amount in Cape Town. Walnuts, raisins, apples, quinces, can all be bought for a mere trifle just now; and if ever we retire to save, we shall certainly go to Worcester.

The town, as I have said, is very prettily planned. The streets are about a mile long, and across each other at right angles, and are planted with double rows of firs, blue gums, and poplars. Each house stands in its own compound, and the gardens are full of roses, and fruit and vegetables, and owe much of their beauty to the admirable system of irrigation adopted by the early Dutch in leading out the waters of the Hex River over the level surface, and, after making the circuit of the streets in small furrows, discharging it again into the Breede River.

It is a town of open thoroughfares and magnificent distances. It has, moreover, a first-rate hotel, where you are made quite at home and thoroughly comfortable.

Worcester today, after the bustle and excitement of Saturday and yesterday, is almost deserted; but on Easter Sunday there was 'Nachtmaal' among the Dutch, and the farmers, with their families flocked in from all the countryside, and quite filled their church. It was curious to see them coming up to the altar, in batches of fifty at a time, to take the Sacrament, all dressed in their black go-to-meeting clothes, and looking so solemn and serious. But a still more interesting sight at Worcester is to attend the service of the Berlin Missionary, who has managed to design and build a very convenient and beautifully-constructed church, quite capable of holding eight hundred people. Its lofty stone spire is quite an ornament to the place, and its windows only require painted glass to be perfect. The singing of the congregation has a very fine effect, and the chants used are very good, but the minister wisely keeps his flock to very simple musical diet. The ventilation of this church is perfect. The women march in at one end, the males at another, while the elders sit crossways in the middle, leaving a wide open space before the altar. I was much impressed by the manifest power wielded by this earnest preacher over his flock of black sheep. His pulpit was a raised platform, enclosed like a bow-window, allowing of considerable movement, and even dramatic action; and as for 'bouquet de natif', I must candidly confess, the odour of sanctity was a great deal more pungent and overpowering in the Dutch church than among these poor labouring people.

Like curious travellers, we spent the greater part of yesterday in attending the different church services, for which the bells of the town were ringing nearly all the day; and in the afternoon we passed a pleasant hour in inspecting the arrangements of the Missionary schools, and learning the history of their foundation and success. They owe everything to Mr. Esselin, who came to this Colony seven years ago, and settled at Worcester in the hope of doing some good amongst the neglected coloured folk. About nine hundred of these poor people were then living at what is now called the 'Location' – a double row of huts and cottages, extending for nearly two miles out of town – and were almost in a state of barbarism; but so hopefully and manfully did he set to work, that in a very short time he had got most of them to attend service pretty regularly, and even display some anxiety to be taught. The church and school were then both held in a rude, thatched building belonging to the Town Council, while their pastor was being supported by the Parent Society at Berlin. After a year or two, he conceived the bold idea of building a church and schools for the especial use of his flock, the expenses to be defrayed by the coloured people themselves. To this end he called a meeting of all the heads of families, and fully entered into the details of his scheme. He then, addressing first the one and then the other by name, fully ascertained from them all what amount of time, labour, or material each one could give towards the erection of the proposed buildings during the ensuing year. As each man came forward with a distinct promise, according to his trade or calling, to carry so much material, quarry so much stone, or do the work of carpenter, mason, or smith for so many days, Mr. Esselin entered the name and all particulars of the public promise into a large book; and then, after adding up the sum total, he determined to draw his own plan, become his own architect, and commence the work without delay. He procured a fine piece of ground, near the market-square, and six months afterwards, with his own hands, he laid the foundation-stone of one of the handsomest, most convenient, and most solidly-built churches in the Colony. It was truly a labour of love. Both pastor and flock worked at it with might and main, and at the end of another six months the final touch was put to this splendid monument of one man's unflagging energy and spirit.

One cannot help being struck by the order and cleanliness of everything connected with this pile of buildings, both within and without. From pulpit to belfry it has been reared by poor men, and owes nothing to charitable support. The church has seats for eight hundred people. On one side sit all the men, decently dressed in black, and with their faces shining as if with the oil of gladness. On the other side are the women, – the old ones in black stuff gowns, with white linen cloths round their poor, grizzled heads, and their withered old faces, placid, and *intensely* respectable, – the mothers of families in long, snow-white 'kappies' hanging down to their shoulders; while the daughters and young girls are without head-covering of any kind, save their own well-combed and occasionally crisp woolly hair. Their singing was singularly sweet and effective, filling the vast space with simple melody. After the service, one old man, whose heart I quite won by praising his church and the singing, confided to me that the great ambition of the congregation was to save up enough to buy a harmonium, and then they thought the singing would be something worth hearing; but on my assuring him that its very simplicity was its present chief charm, he was quite happy and contented. These coloured people have a wonderfully quick ear for music, and their voices are plaintively sweet, but not capable of a very high range. They excel in psalmody.

I learned from the minister, who is a very able, ingenious, and thoroughly well-informed gentleman, that it was not until a year afterwards that they were able to complete the schools. But now – many years after their erection – they look as clean and orderly as if just finished. The white-washed walls are like snow, the arched roof glistens with stained pine, the floor is clean enough to eat from, and shines till you can almost see your face in it. There are four of these schools, built in a sort of quadrangle: one for boys, another for girls, a third for infants, and the fourth for infants of a larger growth.

Arranged in long rows up each side of the hall were the desks and benches, each shining as if they had been newly varnished; whereas they owe all their polish to five years' elbow grease. The infant school was like a little cabinet of curiosities, everything being on the tiniest scale. From the floor up half-way to the ceiling rose tier upon tier of highly-polished little benches, and round the walls were hung every description of bird and beast, well painted; with lessons on colour, on form, – in fact, everything that a child should learn. No English school could be more perfectly furnished!

Wednesday, 23rd April.— On Monday I was quite tired out with sight-seeing and scribbling, and must have walked over an amazing extent of ground, looking at the gardens, tasting fruit, and admiring the flowers. Everybody told us we had come at the worst time of year, and ought to return in September, when the hedges would be full of roses, and the *veldt* blazing with bulbs; but I was more than satisfied with things as they were. Many of the gardens were enclosed with tall hedges of quinces, and the tapering switches of this fruit-tree blossomed like Aaron's rod with myriads of golden balls, most fragrant to smell, and equally pleasant to eat. They make a sort of 'chutnee' out of quinces, which they call '*sambal*', by slicing the fruit into a mortar, adding a pinch of salt and cayenne pepper, and a green chilly minced very fine, and then pounding the whole with a pestle till it is well bruised and reduced to a pulp. Eaten fresh with cold or roast meat, or with curried dishes, it is a capital spur to a jaded appetite, and well worth trying.

Yesterday we made an excursion to Brandt Vlei, or the Boiling Lake, distant about one hour from Worcester, and only to be reached by jolting through the dry and stony bed of Breede River, and bumping our heads off along a most rutty and abominable track. The springs which supply it must be of volcanic origin, for here – wonderful to relate – we saw water of crystalline clearness, but perfectly tasteless, bubbling up in a natural cauldron of twelve feet deep and thirty feet diameter, *within a few yards of a cold spring*. The heat of the water was 140 degrees, and it took two hours to cool it perfectly in a bottle; but it has no medicinal properties. The astonishing thing is, that the vapour and steam from this boiling spring, far from injuring the tropical vegetation hereabouts, apparently improve it, and tufts of grass and pig-lilies and bamboo are actually growing in this very water, as if they liked it. I pulled up some, and found the sand very hot to the touch, and the roots were scalding hot, but each blade was fresh and green. Who can explain this mystery? From these springs – for there are two, one much smaller than the other and not so deep, but apparently communicating, for when we stirred the smaller one up with a long pole, the bigger lake began to bubble up furiously from its bed of silver sand, and sent up thousands of silvery rings to the surface – the water is conveyed away by wooden channels, one of which supplies a bath-house close by, and the other forms the stream which irrigates the vale, and can be traced for many miles, by its smoke and vapour, among the mealies. The farmer to whom the place belongs told us the water was very good for rheumatism, if one could stand being almost boiled alive, and it took an hour at least to cool it to the bathing point; so that, with a trifling expense, there ought to be no difficulty in conveying it direct by pipes to Worcester, and there employing it medicinally, instead of sending invalids all that way in search of fractured bones or dislocations.

On our way back we saw some grotesque objects moving about on all fours near a mealie patch, when our driver gave a shout, and lo and behold! up started a dozen of big baboons, and fled for their lives, chattering and cocking up their ridiculous tails, and carrying off their youngsters on their backs. Somebody pointed his gun at them and was going to fire, but the driver begged so hard that he would desist that he yielded the point at once. It seems the baboons, when wounded, cry like beaten children, and this our poor driver could not stand, – nor I think could you. He told us quite seriously that the baboons always beat most unmercifully the unfortunate sentinel who has failed to keep proper guard while the rest are out stealing, but whether with his own tail or with a special stick he was at a loss to determine. All along these stony hillocks over which the so-called road is carried, there grow very curious euphorbia bushes, called the *butter bush*. If you break off a twig, a thick juice escapes, very sticky, and exactly like newly-churned butter. Here also you find tufts of reed called the '*melkbosch*', which are full of a milky fluid, only grateful to goats, for sheep will not touch it. And, more surprising still, near Brandt Vlei we were shown what was called the 'bread tree', from the supposed resemblance between the taste of its fruit and a very dry crust. Thus these seemingly barren hills are tenanted by baboons who are provided with milk and honey, bread and butter, and as much hot water as would serve for the cooking of everything they could manage to steal! Truly, Nature plays some strange tricks in South Africa.

One marked peculiarity about Worcester is the clearness of its atmosphere. This made the sunsets especially beautiful from the reflected pink and amber lights playing on the lofty crags, when the valleys were in deep shade. Unfortunately for sketchers, these floods 'of radiance unutterably bright' only last a few minutes, whereas at Green Point the effect of a rosy cloud over the setting sun would be to flush the whole sea with amethyst and purple, and make the horizon red as wine. The air here among the mountains is, in fact, too thin and transparent to retain the glow of colour very long, and is undoubtedly a great drawback to sportsmen, who find all kinds of game very wild and difficult to approach. As stalking bucks is quite out of the question, you have to trust to a speedy horse, and gallop in a circle, before you can come near enough to fire. The gentlemen of our party are quite wild with me for admiring the purity of the air, which to them must be just as annoying as the 'stinking violets' complained of by John Leech's Huntsman. Both spoil sport, and are sometimes out of place!

Cape Town, 1st May.— Here we are again in Cape Town, all the better for our trip, and only sorry that we could not have stayed longer in Worcester; but the fact is, the children fretted after us, and so we were obliged to come back, at least a week before our time. *** If there had been a railway in existence, nothing I would have enjoyed more than making up a large party to explore the beauties of the Hex River country; but that terrible long, steep drive for eighteen miles up hill and down through Bain's Kloof, although very beautiful, is too much for human nature, more than once a year. If ever a country calls for railways, it is about Tulbagh and Worcester, where the land is so flat, that a rise of four or five feet in the rivers causes wide plains to be under water; and it is painful to see the poor oxen toiling up the passes with the heavy loads of wine and brandy, sunk up to the axles in mud and sand. If ever a train runs to Worcester, the citizens of Cape Town will make it their favourite suburb; and I, for one, should then like to live there altogether. *** In our absence, nothing fresh had occurred beyond the arrival of race-horses from far and near to compete for the Autumn races, and as yesterday was really a beautiful day, we made up a riding party, and went to see the Cape Town races. The Grand Stand, which is a very humble glazed little box, was pretty well filled, and the *jeunesse dorè* of the Cape turned out in great force; but by far the most amusing feature of the scene was the intense eagerness with which small groups of excited natives backed their noisy opinions in half-crowns and shillings. The racing was comparatively poor, the horses slight, few in number, and not particularly well trained, while the costumes of the jockeys were remarkably bizarre, and sadly deficient in boots; but what astonished us was to see a queer, rough little shooting pony, called *Gazelle*, carry off the 'Queen's Plate' from a noble imported English horse, and this in spite of the very fine riding of an old English jockey against a weazened little Hottentot. When this winner returned to scale, the noise and uproar of the blacks were something prodigious. It was as good as a play to watch their antics. They danced and jumped about, threw up their caps, shook each other by the hands, laughing, crowing, and jeering the jockey who was second, as if he had been detected in doing something shameful. In short, the course was taken possession of by a delirious mob, and had to be cleared by the police. As we were standing close to the weighing paddock, looking on at the horses being led about, it was very amusing to listen to the several critical remarks of these exuberant 'niggers', who know as much about the points of a horse as a cow does about dancing, and to contrast the dignified calm, and quiet demeanour of the jockeys within, with the noisy gestures and uncouth compliments showered on them by their apish and excitable compatriots without. The effervescence of animal spirits was something astonishing!

The races are held on a wide commonage, skirted 'by the sounding sea', with ships passing and repassing to and from the anchorage, and fanned by breezes both salt and pleasant. They seemed to be regarded by most people as an excuse for picnics on the rocks; and the course was inconveniently full of family groups, who, seated in carts, or *under* them, found their hampers all too small for the friends who came crowding to the open-air feast. Turf there was none, but rather a coarse mixture of sand and rank growths, combining the softness of moss with the dryness of straw, and one likely to tire out the strongest horse after a little hard galloping. The course is nearly oval, and is traced out by a line of houses and seaside villas, whose white-washed walls stand out brilliantly against the background of dark-blue sea and overhanging hills and we had some capital scampers across it between the races. When all was over, the scene upon the road home was almost as amusing as the Derby Return. Carts, full of Malay families, dressed in all the colours of the rainbow, and with gowns that positively were *prismatic*, went racing back to town at imminent risk of upsetting their contents, and setting off the horses of quieter gentry into paroxysms of kicking. Roads, common, and side-walks were crammed by a motley and eager crowd, pushing, struggling, and jostling their way on foot so as to keep up with the bands of fiddlers in caravans, who were playing lively dance music; while along the hillside, high above our heads, might be discerned small groups of nervous females, who had brought themselves to anchor in such out-of-the-way spots rather than lose taking a share in a spectacle which to passengers just entering the Bay must present a very busy and unique appearance.

Sunday, 11th May.— The fact of our having shortly to leave for the frontier, has again unsettled our household, and made us the victims of caprice. What a nuisance it is, this constant shifting from one place to another, when anybody could have done the work so much better than ourselves! The waste of time by dawdling about in an hotel would be unbearable, were it not for the resources of the free Library here, which in its cool and spacious apartments offers attractions second to none in Cape Town. If ever you were to come here, you would soon agree with me that it combines the convenience of the British Museum with the advantages of Mudie's, and is one of the cheapest luxuries within the reach of the British soldier, costing next to nothing.

Once a year it is the custom of the committee to invite the most prominent member of the Cape Town society with a turn for literature to deliver an address in connection with this Institute, and then all the blue-stockings muster in great force to hear themselves well praised, and to take their share in the proceedings of a mutual admiration society. Yesterday the choice of the subscribers fell upon Mr. John F—, who is regarded in South Africa as the father of the Press, and is mentioned elsewhere by Pringle. *** The old man seemed in very weak health, and quite unfit to plead before the blooming jury of smartly-dressed women who crowded the big hall of the Library; but his looks belied him, and he delivered an address quite instinct with true genius, and of which I shall hereafter send you a copy when it is printed. The proceedings were marked by an incident which made a powerful impression on my mind, and gave me a good idea of the startling effects to be got out of an apt quotation when forcibly delivered. Just as the meeting was breaking up the dear old Attorney-General rose to move a vote of thanks, and after a most brilliant eulogium on the career of the speaker, and reference to the fact that he himself was too broken down in health to do justice to his theme, and might probably never again have the pleasure of meeting the man who had so long been his guide, philosopher, and friend, he wound up his remarks by saying, with, oh! such tender pathos and delicious thrilling tones, that the words are still ringing in my ears: 'Wealth decays, and rank is nothing', –

'But strew his ashes to the wind
Whose sword or voice has served mankind;
And *is he dead*; whose glorious mind
Lifts him on high?
To *live* in hearts we leave behind
Is *not* to die!'

To have heard these touching words from one grey-headed man to another, may to you, at a distance, seem as nothing; but to us on the spot, with the mind's eye full of a colossal form and a gracious presence, there was something almost tragic in this eloquent farewell. Eveybody knows, of course, that the speaker was on the eve of leaving for England, and was deeply attached to his many friends at the Cape, so it was only natural he should feel the hour of parting; but no one could have watched that strong and handsome face quivering with emotion in every feature, without being struck by the godlike air with which these lines were delivered. It was electrifying. I would not have missed that scene for a good deal, nor yet the equally touching scene later in the day, when Mr. P— went on board the *Camperdown*, and was accompanied all the way down the streets to the wharf by a tremendous crowd of well-wishers, who never seemed tired of shaking hands and saying good-bye to him, as he strode on, silent, downcast, and thoroughly overcome. The bay that day was gay with large boats filled with Volunteers, as with bands playing and flags flying they escorted their popular Colonel to the ship. It is not permitted to all to so leave a Colony, after a residence of a quarter of a century – perhaps never to return! I wonder how many people in England would so greet the most popular man of the day, who had deserved well of his country; or would they not be somewhat ashamed of such warm-heartedness, and sneer at this southern fervour and vivacity of friendship.

CHAPTER TEN

Silver leaves and a State Ball

18th May, 1862

This is just the sort of house that I would like to be mistress of – being cool, airy, and well sheltered by trees, only wanting a colony of rooks to make it perfect, and heaps of friends to share one's hospitality. Failing these, I have been killing time this week by gadding about town in search of curiosities to send home by the *Briton*. As I have not got too much money to spare, you must tender my apologies to all friends who expect solid remembrances from the Cape for the trifling value of the articles I am sending to your address; but as some of them are very pretty notwithstanding, they must learn to be content. Many of the things are rudely made up; but that you can easily rectify. In the tin box you will find rolled up a fancy tablecover made out of patches of penguin skin, most tastefully sewn together in a wheel pattern. It will do famously for your round little tea-table, and only requires to be quilted on to some blue or red cloth, to show off its velvety grey, black, and orange plumage to advantage. At least fifty birds must have been destroyed to provide this intricate little bit, as the only portions used in the manufacture are the back, the breast, and the side of the neck. It is shocking waste of material; but then *que voulez vous*, when they are annually breeding in thousands. *** By the merest chance I came across the lovely grey 'duiker' skin, which I intend for Aunt M—. It was given to me by a lady, whose husband had shot the buck from which it was stripped; and so carefully has it been removed that everything is perfect, down to the hoofs, muzzle, and ears. You must have it damped to take out the creases, and then stretched on a piece of bright scarlet cloth, so as to form a soft anti-macassar for her reading chair. *** The 'veldt-kombaars', or sheep-skin rug, in which the shepherds camp out at night, is made out of little squares of lamb skin, and is sewn together by natives, who have a great knack at this kind of fancy work: and you must please present it to old Mrs.— of D—, as a carriage rug. It has no smell, and will harbour no fleas, and will, besides, be warmer than three blankets. *** In the little biscuit-box I have packed away a regular set of Cape jewellery, consisting of two bracelets, a necklace, earrings, brooch, and a waistbelt, all formed out of beads and the delicate seeds of the tiny musk-melon. When worn at night they have all the appearance of *dead gold*, and I am sure they will look famously on your little cousin K—. They are made by the farmers' daughters for their amusement, and cost a mere trifle. At one of the shops, I was shown some beautiful things in Indian silver filagree, in the way of card cases and bracelets, but they are too delicate and expensive, and I am afraid will tarnish in your moist neighbourhood, and consequently require to be burnished anew; but the patterns of these toys are exquisitely fine, and well worthy of being reproduced in gold. In a wild burst of extravagance, I bought a lot of book-markers made out of silver-leaves, glazed in some way, and then painted in water-colours, with sketches of native figures. *** You can divide a dozen of these at your discretion between the B—s and the L—s factions; and reserve the best engraved ostrich egg for yourself. If cut in two, rimmed with silver, and then mounted on a boxwood pedestal, it would make a pretty flower vase for your table.

Apropos of silver-leaves – if you will take the trouble to bind them with a narrow edging of blue or red satin ribbon, and arrange them like the sun's rays in points, on four bits of card-board, covered with silk, you will make a very pretty work-box out of the sheaf I herewith send you from Silver Tree Hill. They will also plait into very neat checquer-work, and are very flexible in the handling. A thin coating of isinglass or size will enable you to paint upon them, and I should think you might even make a fan out of them. The funniest use I ever saw them put to was at a ball, where a young arrival, enchanted with their lustre, tacked them on to her skirt, and made herself look supremely ridiculous, as they were ruthlessly stripped off and strewn about the room in the mad rush of excited waltzers. *** The sugar-birds and humming-birds, about which you wrote to me, are getting very scarce now, and are only to be shot with great trouble near the Black River on the Cape Flats. Those I send you have been prepared with arsenical soap by Mr. R—T—, a very good-natured young fellow, who is awfully clever at beetles and butterflies, and who has really been most obliging in getting me good specimens to send home to you all for wearing in your hats. He was kind enough also to give me the lovely 'lourie' wing, which he tells me is obtained from a rare bird in the Knysna forests, that has the merit of having baffled all naturalists hitherto as to its mode of breeding and making its nest, &c. When flying in the sun, they glitter all over like burnished metal with the lustrous green and deep claret hues of their feathers. I intend this for Sophy's riding hat, and I hope she will take good care of it. Give the two red and black Kafir finches to old Mrs.—: they will serve to brighten up her best bonnet. *** I have had the tiny shells of the little 'schoelpats', or water-tortoises, slightly lacquered. They are used by some natives to hold money and snuff. You can easily fit them anew with heads and feet of velvet, being cold-blooded animals, and use them as paper weights.

As for the bunches of the different kinds of grasses that you will find sewn up in a bag, they were collected by us in our travels over Bain's Kloof and near Worcester; and if appropriately dyed and mixed up with the glittering pink and yellow everlasting flowers found near Wellington, will compose into very pretty flat bouquets, mounted on sheets of thick cardboard with pearly shells and seaweed. To show you what I mean, I send you a few specimens of this kind of ornamental work, and they are so tastefully arranged by some of the poorer ladies here, that it will puzzle you to improve on them. That particular species of brown grass, which glistens like bronze, retains its lustre for years, and grows all over the Tulbagh district, and contrasts well with the vivid colours of the everlasting flowers. These cards range in price from five to fifteen shillings, according to size, and are very pretty when framed. They are nice things of a fancy bazaar. In the way of sticks, my husband has made a unique collection, – the oddest one being not unlike an enormous gimlet, from the action of a creeping parasite that clings to it like a leech and scores the bark deeply; while the most elaborate one he has was carved out of a piece of driftwood by a Kafir chief imprisoned on Robben Island. He has also got a stick for Robert, with big thorns spirally arranged at every two inches, and a most uncomfortable one to walk with in company. If it could be managed, he ought to send him a real Cape bamboo stick, to show how the Malays fish and drive with it, but as it would be nearly twenty feet long, and cannot be jointed or taken to pieces, tapering from the thickness of a gun-barrel to the point of a whip, I am afraid we must forego that pleasure; but I send you instead the lash that ought to be fastened to it. It is over thirty feet long, and carefully plaited by the natives, and, if well wielded, makes a greater noise than the short-handled Australian stock-whip, of which we hear so much in the papers. Let Uncle John have it. The last thing in the box will puzzle you all tremendously. It is a pair of Malay sandals, and is herewith presented to any of you who can clutch them tightly with the great toe, and hobble across the room without breaking his neck. They will remind you of Mr. Winkle's first attempts at skating without a chair to steady him. *** Of course, I could have made the parcel larger by buying Kafir pipes, snuff-pouches, and bead aprons, &c.; but I prefer to pick up these articles from the veritable savages themselves when once we get to the Frontier, and our departure now cannot be much longer delayed. *** In the meantime, take the goods the Gods provide you, though lovely Thais *don't* sit beside you.

Friday, 30th May.— We are still at this hotel, and likely to remain so till the middle of next month. The suspense is tiresome, and we are spending more money than we bargained for while waiting for a ship; but, otherwise, we are enjoying the winter very much. For a place with so few public amusements or theatres, we have been unusually gay this week, for on Tuesday the Queen's birthday was celebrated by a Regatta, followed in the evening by a State Ball, – the weather throughout being all that could be desired at this pleasant but showery and fickle time of year. At all events, everybody seemed to be in very good spirits out-of-doors, for the morning was fine, bright, and bracing, the sky without a cloud, and a smart breeze blowing into Table Bay from the west. Even so, Cape Town in winter is not very cold; but if no wind is stirring, it is truly enchanting and delicious to get out and bask in the sunshine that floods the whole town, after a shower of rain has settled the dust and cleared the air. Before the opening of the Regatta, all the world and his wife and picaninnies were collected on the Grand Parade – a big but much neglected square, about a quarter of a mile long – to see the troops in garrison reviewed by the Governor and his Staff, and to stare at the military evolutions, and the firing of the *feu de joie* from the Castle ramparts. A handful of Volunteers – artillery, cavalry, and riflemen – also went through some scrambling performances in the presence of at least six thousand amused spectators, and I am not sure that their dignified march past was not the best of the day's fun, – so clearly were the fat men in the ranks out of condition, and unable to keep step together, in spite of the hoarse entreaties from the agonized officers.

After this was over, and the little black boys had picked up the half-exploded cartridges – almost at the very mouths of the rifles, careless of consequences – everybody rushed down to the wharves and Central Jetty, to gape with astonishment at the lively and eccentric movements of the innumerable boats and wherries that were plying about between the shipping and the shores of Table Bay. Wherever it was possible to have a flag flying, there you saw it fluttering in the breeze, which at first had threatened to be a litte too rough; but about one o'clock it died away, and the wind and sea became more favourable, so that it was quite pleasant to watch the crews of the Malay whale and fishing-boats darting about from point to point like gigantic dragon-flies. As all the wharves and elevated spots were crowded by the holiday-loving spectators, you may fancy how the swarms of the gaily-dressed children and their gorgeously attired parents made the scene lively beyond description. To me, the prettiest sight was the race between the fishermen's luggers. It was closely contested half-way round the bay, and the winner owed his victory apparently to the fact of his men constantly dashing buckets of sea water over his sails, so as to make them draw better, I suppose. Later in the day it became very cold on the wharves, and the spray stung my face like a thousand pin points. And here I may say, that although this sudden change from summer to winter leaves the sky as bright and blue as ever, yet it makes its influence felt in the shortness of the daylight, – it being nearly dark at half-past five, greater dampness at night, and a decided sense of chilliness out-of-doors. There is no ice, and many people insist upon it that what some call snow upon the hills opposite is only packed hail. When it does rain, however, it comes down in buckets full, keeping on steadily for hours, making big rivers out of narrow street-gutters, and churning the soft material of the miserable roadways into vast sheets of mud, so that walking about after a shower or two is a very splashy adventure indeed, but a very enjoyable one, nevertheless, on account of the balmy freshness and crispness of the air, when the sun shines out again.

After the Regatta, there was a State Ball given by the Governor and Mrs. Wodehouse, to all who had duly left their cards at Government-house for at least twice in the season, and at which over three hundred people were present, including the garrison, as well as the officers of the *Cossack* and *Narcissus*, &c., &c. There happened to be a good many war-ships just then at Simon's Bay, chiefly foreigners, so that there was no lack of epaulettes and blue jackets to keep the fun going till three in the morning. The rooms, being very large as well as lofty, were not inconveniently full, and the whole affair was very gay, and would have been even more appreciable, had it been for the manner in which the dancers got all jumbled up together, by all attempting to dance at once, and so treading upon each other's toes most painfully in the waltzes and galops. The marked absence of any master of the ceremonies caused everybody to jostle his fair neighbours, quite politely and good-humouredly, it is true, but still a strip of carpeting round the room would have defined a neutral ground upon which no dancers could have intruded, and then those who were waiting their turn could not have so hampered others who were dancing for their amusement.

The good old German plan of three turns round the room and then a pause would have given everybody in succession a chance of trotting out his partner, without thumping her shoulders blue, or tearing her dress to pieces. Another great drawback at Government-house was the want of recognized stewards or aides-de-camp in waiting to introduce strangers to suitable partners. This must make it very embarrassing to naval men, here today and gone tomorrow, who are specially fond of dancing, and thoroughly enjoy a hearty romp ashore in the lancers or the galop; but who, because there is no official to find them ladies, keep crowding round the folding doors and obstructing the passages to and from the drawing-room.

Most of the dresses were in good taste, not too much *decolletè*, and fitting very well. Here and there I saw traces of Parisian millinery, but on the whole, I suspect very few dressmakers were employed, except at home; and that many of the ladies were not in the habit of going out to balls more than once in the year. That air of *je ne sais quoi* which marks the habitué of good society was not to my eye so *prononcé* in the company as I could have wished, and a little judicious weeding of the invitations would have made the assembly more at ease with each other. Many of the stranger faces were very pretty, and two sisters with black hair were pointed out to me who would have done honour to any court by their figures and graceful carriage. The belle of the ball was a lovely young girl in green tarlatan – Dutch by birth – French in style, with most bewitching eyes and shoulders. The dancing of all was surprisingly good. It was wonderful to witness the ease and lightness with which large massive-looking matrons were wafted round the room in perfect accord with the music by the foreign officers; in charming contrast to the giddy pace at which more sylph-like figures were spun and swung along over the slippery floor by our more manly but far less elegant subalterns. Here all grace and elegance, there the haste and rudeness of school-boys to be first.

Our host, as Her Majesty's representative, was dressed in his Windsor uniform, and wore his star and ribbon. He is a portly, haughty middle-aged gentleman of good presence, but rather hard-featured. He has the character of being a hard rider, but to me his movements were jerky and stiff, and constrained, as if his coat was too tight for him. Like all Governors, he has lots of work to go through; but he does not promise to be as popular as old Sir George Grey, who was as thin as a lath, and shambled in his walk, but who was full of urbanity and old-fashioned politeness, and who always had a kind word to say to everybody – even to the wall flowers – and liked to know the ins and outs of every household. *** Mrs. Wodehouse, however, is a dear, sweet-faced old lady, with streaks of gray in her hair, a nervous, frightened manner, and with delicate sensitive features, that invite one's confidence and respect. She just moved through a quadrille or two, and has the credit of being very well read and passionately attached to her husband. She spent the greater portion of the evening on the sofa, placed on the raised dais at the top of the ball-room, quite under the music gallery, talking to the wives of the various judges and secretaries, &c. This is the only sign of ceremonial, so that a state ball at the Cape is not heavy with etiquette, but is quite as easy and unconstrained as any private party. When supper was announced at twelve o'clock precisely, the guests filed in in the order of precedence, and then when the big-wigs and their ladies were seated, humbler folk like ourselves were allowed to fill up the banqueting-hall, and clear the well-furnished tables as often as they pleased. There was only one toast given, namely 'The Queen'; and on the whole, people seemed to buzz and enjoy themselves all the more after the champagne bottles in dozens had been set popping in every direction. As far as the style of the supper went, nothing could have been done in better taste.

Monday, 9th June.— I have been wearing my legs off today in wandering about the old Castle, trying to find out the quarters of various acquaintances, so as to say good-bye. When first we came here, many of our friends lived in the front square, and could be traced up without much trouble; but of late there have been so many changes and removals that you require to have the strength of Samson and the patience of Job to ferret them out of the wretched dens in which the Quartermaster-General's Department have now buried them alive.

To give you some idea of the miseries of military life when you are poor or of inferior rank, let me tell you of my day's adventures, and then say whether you envy the unfortunates who have to sniff the odours of that pleasant wet ditch, or moat, or whatever they choose to call it, that distributes mud round three sides of the Castle. No wonder, as a rule, that Castle divinities look pale and fagged, and are always sending for the doctor, for I am sure they are lodged worse than wild beasts, and merit our pity. To get at the first name on my list, I had to make many inquiries from stupid sentries and not over civil slatternly soldier-servants hanging about, until I was at length directed to a dreary inner court-yard, cold as a church, and with its flags and rough stones overgrown with moss and lichen, as if the sun never peeped into it from year's end to year's end. Here, on the left, were some barracks, where a number of half-dressed men were lounging about and smoking, and making the air ring again with their coarse jokes and laughter. Turning, as directed, quickly off to the right, and stumbling over a number of rough uneven stones, I found myself staring at a door, with a calling-card nailed to it, but so filthy and weather-beaten that at first I thought I must be wrong, and that it must be one of the stable-doors, as it was close alongside of the dirtiest place possible for even horses to be stabled in. Across the path meandered a stream of greenish hue, not very thick or broad, but oh! very, very strong indeed in scent. With my pocket handkerchief to my nose, and my petticoats well gathered up, I jumped across this, and entering the said doorway and looking about for a bell or knocker and finding none, I had to toil up a dirty stone staircase – every footstep echoing noisily through the vaulted passages. Over my head was suspended a delicate drapery of cobwebs, evidently of many years' standing – or rather hanging, so that I felt rather a creeping sensation on the top of my head lest one of their huge hairy occupants should suddenly drop down upon me. Arrived at the head of the stairs I stood bewildered, for four passages extended away in different directions, and which was I to take? At last, above my head, about half a dozen steps up – I saw a door which looked promising – so at once posted up to it. Imagine my horror when I read the card tacked to it, and found I had intruded into bachelors' quarters! Of course, I hurried down quicker than I came up, trusting that no one had seen me; but I need not have feared, as the place was as damp, silent, and deserted as a huge vault. Not a figure moved, not a sound was to be heard! At last, in despair I made a dash down the opposite passage and actually found the door I wanted, but I could get nobody to attend to it. After banging away at it until I broke my parasol, and nearly lost my temper, I just

poked a p.p.c. card under it and retreated. Right glad was I to emerge again into the sunshine, as I was chilled to the bone, and carried a nice fringe of straw and dust on my black silk dress.

Then nothing would satisfy me but I must go and hunt up Mrs.—, who, though her quarters are not so inaccessible as Mrs.—'s, commands a cheerful view of a blank brown wall rising up just in front of her drawing-room window! Being a woman of taste, she does not shudder at the difficulties in the way of making her rooms look a little home-like; but what with the want of papering, the scarcity of paint, and the trouble of hanging up pictures against whitewashed walls except on screens and framed stands – her scanty furniture wore an inexpressibly dreary air, as if an execution was in the house, and it was not worth tidying up. *** Then, though getting very tired, I tried my luck again, and in search of No. 3 on my list toiled up and up, from one flight of stairs to another flight of stairs – past one lady's kitchen, where afternoon tea was going on amongst a select circle of servants and their friends, – past another's wood and fowl-house, – and so on and on, until I emerged upon the ramparts, where I sat down for a few minutes on the roof of one of the houses, to enjoy the beautiful view of the town and bay, looking so bright and cheerful in the sunlight. However, it was no time for dawdling, so up I jumped, and was nearly frightened out of my wits by the sudden appearance of a huge baboon, who emerged from behind one of the chimneys, rattling his chain, showing his ugly teeth, and barking at me. You could have knocked me over with a feather! Recovering myself, I fled down six more steps, past a water tank, round a corner into a passage where the front door faced the open door of the kitchen, and then I sank down, only too grateful at having accomplished my duties so far, and well rewarded by the offer of a nice cup of tea.

This experience will give you a fair idea of what the holes and corners of the Castle consist of. Some are worse and some are better; but with the exception of the Commandant's and General's quarters, and one or two good rooms overlooking the bay, you may take my word for it that these dens are scarcely fit to give shelter to a donkey, much less ladies and children. The tiniest little cottage of four rooms and a kitchen has a great deal more comfort in it; and catch me again taking up my residence in a hurry where you can't hammer a nail, or get a pane of glass put in, without frightful fuss and a long correspondence with a Department. *** And yet these nests of abomination and discomfort, so disgraceful to the authorities, could be made very different, if a little painting and doing up were sanctioned, some trees planted about, fire-places provided, and some provision made for securing decent ventilation and suitable approaches from any of the court-yards. If I were the General commanding out here, I would precious soon level and re-grass the parades, clean out the moat, encourage gardening on the ramparts, and put the place into something like order, with the aid of soldiers, who are idly loafing about in the meantime, doing nothing but cleaning arms, and drinking cheap wine and brandy.

Saturday, 14th June.— At last we have taken our passages in the *Waldensian*, and we were going to send our horses on overland to Graham's Town – some five hundred miles off, but the heavy rains and stormy weather have so affected the rivers that we have been advised to ship them in the same streamer with ourselves. I hear horses on the Frontier are not so docile, and are smaller than those near Cape Town, and I am loath to be parted from my dear little 'Sunbeam'. But everything else we have sent to the public sales, so as to start afresh in housekeeping. Nothing can exceed the ease and readiness with which people get rid of property here. You put a short advertisement into the papers that you are going to sell off on such and such a day, and upon the day in question, if it is fine, all the world and his wife in their carriages will flock to your house, which is open to all corners, and after minutely criticizing all your household arrangements, and distributing themselves over your chairs, ottomans, and sofas – just as they stand – there they will patiently sit as if at a reception, until the auctioneer enters the room, and sells off everything amidst enthusiastic competition. The excitement of a sale and the bidding of a rival will often cause people to give fabulous prices for the simplest little thing. The auctioneer moves in the best society, knows everybody, cracks his dry jokes, and tries to suit all tastes with wonderful accuracy and tact. I have seen as many as two hundred people crowded into every room of a big house, all eagerly bent on picking up bargains, and buying a great many more things than they know what to do with, and every now and then you hear a roar of laughter as the auctioneer knocks down an article at three times its real value. Books, carpets, flowers in pots, and pictures move off as if by magic. Tables, beds, and knick-knacks rapidly vanish, and in less than three hours the establishment is about cleared out. Then everybody adjourns to a well-spread lunch of sandwiches and bottled ale set out in some quiet passage or under the trees, and discusses it at the expense of the owner of the property, after which the purchasers very probably bid more furiously than ever!

If a house has to be sold, it is done in the funniest way possible. The auctioneer walks about with a bag of gold in one hand and a roll of bank-notes in the other, and keeps shouting out, 'Who says *two* thousand pounds for this splendid house and grounds? Will nobody make me an offer? Well then here's ten pounds for whoever says *fifteen* hundred pounds?' Still no answer! Everybody looks unconcernedly at his neighbour, as if the sum was a matter of perfect indifference. At last, the auctioneer, says, 'Say *fourteen* hundred, and here's ten pounds!' and at once half a dozen hands are thrust out to receive it. Somebody takes the money, and now the sale commences *in earnest*. This is now a real *bonâ fide* bid, and, unless the persons who gave and took the bribe can induce anybody to make an advance on the price, the house is sold. But then comes the fun, to watch the anxious looks of some poor needy wretch who is dying to get rid of his bargain, but still retain his bribe. Again and again the auctioneer walks round and round, peering into the face of one, and whispering slyly into the ear of another, till at last he says, 'Well, then, I will give twenty pounds to whoever says *fifteen* hundred and fifty pounds!' Again somebody silently snatches at the bonus, to the intense delight of the holder of the first ten pounds given away, for he is *now relieved of all responsibility*, and can walk home thoroughly well satisfied with his day's earnings. And so the gambling goes on until the property is forced up to the required price, every bonus being a free gift, except the one last taken. Houses are thus often sold for more than they really are worth; but the Dutch are very fond of this pastime, and it must require much nerve and knowledge of the value of property everywhere to join in it long, without burning one's fingers. When once the house is knocked down to you, you sign a paper, get the sale registered, pay some transfer fees, and there you are – a Cape householder at once!

At the public auctions on the Parade every Saturday, things are managed a little differently. Everybody sends to these sales whatever they want to get rid of, and, of course, a note to the auctioneer as well. He just sells off everything without reserve to the highest bidder – from a pigeon to an elephant, and at the end of the week you call for a cheque – less commission charges, and you have no further trouble in the matter. Hence auctioneers, from the largeness of their transactions, are obliged to command considerable wealth, and, in fact, are very important personages. These Saturday Sales are quite a Cape institution, and include the funniest mixture of articles imaginable. They would be a blessing to every English town where they were established, and at once do away with low pawnbrokers for the poor and needy. I once asked an auctioneer what was the funniest thing he had ever seen sold, and he told me that he 'had known of an auctioneer who was so keen that he had sold the pot from off the fire, *with the Irish stew in it*, rather than be cheated out of his rents!' This, I think, will give you some idea of what people will buy at the Cape on the Grand Parade on a Saturday, if it looks like a bargain! I have reason to speak well of these sales, as we got capital prices for the veriest rubbish that somehow had got into our possession, and which I was willing to have paid people to have carted away for nothing.

Thursday, 19th June.— I have just time to say that we have got everything on board, and that we sail some time this evening. The horses are in boxes on deck, and in three days' time we shall be at Port Elizabeth. Till then, adieu! What will the future have in store for us? Is it possible that people on the frontier can be kinder than people down here? If so, we shall have a merry time of it.

PUBLISHER'S POSTSCRIPT

Who was the lady?

*T*hese enchanting vignettes entitled Life at the Cape, By a Lady, *vividly describing life in Cape Town during the years 1861–2, appeared in Volumes I, II and III of* the Cape Monthly Magazine, New Series. *This revival of the* Cape Monthly Magazine *appeared from 1870 until 1879, and was edited by Prof. Noble. Volume I covered the period July to December 1870; Volume II from January to June 1871; and Volume III from July to December of that year.*

The editor introduced the articles in a footnote to the first, which appeared in August 1870. "By the kindness of an old friend, we have been favoured with a perusal of a batch of unpublished letters from the Cape, written by a lady who took a deep interest in all things appertaining to the Colony, while stationed here ten years ago with her husband the late Captain B——. They show us in our true colours; and seem worthy of an extended circulation. We shall continue to publish them from time to time as occasion may warrant." 'The Lady's' first letter was dated 'Cape Town, Castle, 20th August, 1861' and signed with the initials 'S.G.B.'

In the preface to Volume II dated January to June 1871, the editor offered a further batch of letters. "We may particularly mention that of the Lady's Letters, which have delightfully descanted upon 'Life at the Cape,' and we hope we have not yet come to an end. Seeing the thorough appreciation with which the first batch of them, that chanced to fall into our possession, was received, we have made timely arrangements to have transmitted to us by an early mail, the continuation of them, which we have reason to believe are still in existence and will be forthcoming in due time. We understand that these will bear special reference to our fair and lively friend's experiences of life on the Eastern frontier, where she proceeded thither some nine years ago."

Unmasking 'The Lady's' identity was undoubtedly a serious business with Prof. Noble's readers; they were given only sufficient clues to keep the trail warm. Thus we know from the letters themselves that she arrived in Cape Town on the Sunday just prior to the date of her first caesurie (20th August 1861); that her sons' names appear to have been Charles and Freddie; that her husband, John or possibly James, B— was an army officer of fairly high rank; and that she and her family left Cape Town on June 19th, 1862 in the Waldensian *bound for Port Elizabeth, her ultimate destination being Grahamstown. The* Waldensian *undoubtedly left Cape Town on June 19th arriving at Port Elizabeth three days later. Both the* Eastern Province Herald *of June 24th, 1862 and the* Grahamstown Journal *of June 28th, printed the passenger list. Those landing at Port Elizabeth were a Mrs. Arbouin with her three daughters and son Raymond; Mr. and Mrs. Solomon and five children plus servant; Mrs. Middleton Bowker; Rev. and Mrs. Cooinack; Mr. and Mrs. Armstrong; Mr. and Mrs. Southey; and several male passengers travelling on their own. A Lieut.-Colonel White was embarking at East London and Mr. and Mrs. Golle and their four children were going to Natal.*

Who then was 'The Lady'? Was she one of the above-named passengers on the Waldensian*? Mr. A.C. Lloyd in an article entitled Some Secrets of South African literature in the* South African Bookman, *No. 4 of December 1911, has this to say about her. "Before leaving anonymous descriptions of former South African society, I may recall the series of letters which ran for some time in the* Cape Monthly Magazine *during 1870, under the title 'Life at the Cape, by a Lady'. The authorship of these letters, which I am assured, formed a faithful picture, gave rise to much speculation, and various ladies were credited with writing them. In fact the earlier ones were written by Mrs. Ross, those from Grahamstown by Mrs. Glanville and those from Natal by Sir John Robinson."*

Mrs. Ross's husband was Dr. W. H. Ross, co-editor with Prof. Noble of the Cape Monthly Magazine, *which strengthens her claim to being the mysterious writer. Certainly the three series of articles show internal evidence of having been written by three different hands. Yet nothing definite has been proved and the modern reader's curiosity is as unsatisfied as that of his 19th Century counterpart. 'S.G.B.' still keeps her secret; and her letters still charm and intrigue with their perceptive, unadorned, picture of a past age.*